TIME WELL SPENT

Memories of a former apprentice motor fitter working for the railways in Birmingham
1957-1963

by

KENNETH C. RYELAND

Ogun's Fire

An Ogun's Fire Book

Copyright © Kenneth C. Ryeland 2016

Cover design & plan by A. Roberts ©

Cover Photograph: The Bill Aldridge Collection
A fitter and his apprentice removing the engine from a British Railways' (London Midland Region) Scammell Scarab. Circa 1957.

All rights reserved. No part of this publication may be reproduced, stored in a retrieval system, or transmitted in any form or by any means, electronic, mechanical, photocopy, recording or otherwise, without prior written permission of the copyright owner. Nor can it be circulated in any form of binding or cover other than that in which it is published and without similar condition including this condition being imposed on a subsequent purchaser.

ISBN 978-1-326-61273-3

For the men and women of the RMED Saltley

BY THE SAME AUTHOR

The Up-Country Man
A personal account of the first one hundred days inside secessionist Biafra. (Memoir)

Tribal Gathering
Eight stories set in 1960s post-colonial West Africa. (Fiction)

The Last Bature
A policeman's tale set in 1960s post-colonial West Africa. (Fiction)

The Mine
A political thriller set in 1960s post-colonial West Africa. (Fiction)

Contents

Diagram:	The RMED Workshops Saltley	vi
Introduction:	Time Well Spent	vii
Chapter 1:	How it all Began	1
Chapter 2:	My First Day	12
Chapter 3:	The British Railways Road Vehicle Fleet	21
	The Next Twenty-One Months: April 57-Jan 59	23
Chapter 4:	The Stores	24
Chapter 5:	Making Friends and Enemies	28
Chapter 6:	The Radiator Cage	31
Chapter 7:	The Electricians/Battery Cage	34
Chapter 8:	Book Learning	40
Chapter 9:	I Become Mobile	43
Chapter 10:	The Tyre Cage	45
Chapter 11:	The Welding Cage	48
Chapter 12:	The Machine Shop	51
Chapter 13:	An Unfortunate Occurrence	54
Chapter 14:	My Day as a Driver's Mate	58
	The Next Thirty-Six Months: Jan 59-Jan 62	62
Chapter 15:	The Engine Overhaul Workshop	63
Chapter 16:	A Disturbing Incident	67
Chapter 17:	The Gearbox and Transmission Workshop	70
Chapter 18:	A Note About National Service (Conscription)	72
Chapter 19:	The Complete Vehicle Overhaul Workshop	74
Chapter 20:	Tragedy Strikes	78
Chapter 21:	The Service and Repair Workshop	81
Chapter 22:	I Get Married	88
	The Final Fifteen Months: Jan 62-April 63	89
Chapter 23:	The District Workshops	90
Chapter 24:	I Finish My Time	95
Chapter 25:	I Leave the Railways	99
Chapter 26:	Was it all Worth it?	100

1605

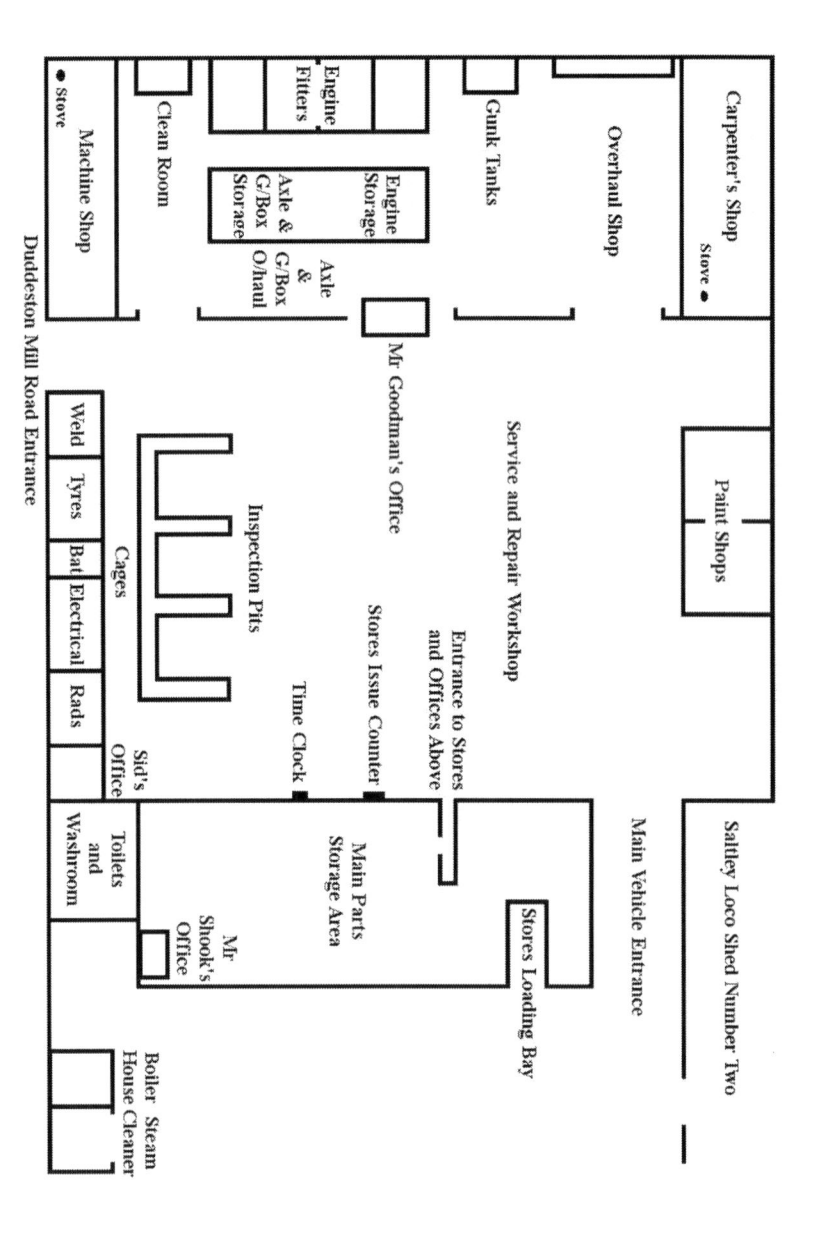

British Railways Road Motor Engineer's Department Workshops at Saltley, Birmingham 1957

INTRODUCTION

When the time came for me to leave school at the age of 15, my parents asked me what I wanted to do regarding a job. I had realised many months before that sooner or later I would have to face this question and provide an answer. I hesitated for a moment and then disclosed that I wanted to do something practical since I was not comfortable with things academic. It was then that my father said, "You can do anything you like, lad, as long as it's a recognised trade and you serve a proper indentured apprenticeship."

Dad had been an indentured apprentice to an electrical engineer in his native North Wales in the late 1920s and early 30s. Later, after finishing his time, he worked for the Central Electricity Generating Board as a linesman, maintaining and repairing the National Grid's high voltage overhead power cables in very remote and inhospitable places.

I didn't realise the significance his words would have on my life until much later in my journey through the world of work, long after my father's death.

Kenneth C. Ryeland
April 2016, Berkshire, England.

Chapter 1
HOW IT ALL BEGAN

I was born in the front bedroom of Nana's house (my maternal grandmother) at number 13, Frederick Road, Stechford, in the eastern suburbs of that great industrial city, Birmingham. It was often referred to as 'The Workshop of the World', 'The City of a Thousand Trades' or, as the locals called it, just plain old 'Brummagem'.

Situated in the very heart of England, the city was known the world over for its skilled workers and their ability to manufacture everything from a pin to a locomotive.

My mother told me later that at the actual time of my entrance to this world there was an air raid going on. It was April 1942 and the Germans were yet again targeting the railway shunting yards and factories that lined the railway track in that part of Stechford.

The Birmingham blitz began on the 9th of August 1940 and continued until the 22nd of April 1944, during which time almost 2,000 tons of high explosives had been dropped on the city causing 2,200 deaths, 6,700 injuries, of which 3,000 were very serious, and the destruction of 12,500 houses, 300 factories and 250 other large buildings. Only London and Liverpool were hit harder by the Luftwaffe during the war. To put these figures into perspective, the population of the city in 1939 was just under one million souls and it was designated the second city of the Empire.

In 1942, my father was a maintenance electrician and this was classified as a reserved occupation by the authorities at that time. He worked at Parkinson, the gas cooker manufacturer situated on nearby Station Road, next to the main London to Birmingham railway line. During the war of course, the factory's output was not gas cookers, but munitions and gun parts. At the moment of my birth, Dad was on fire-watching duty, together with a couple of other employees, on the roof of the factory ready with his bucket of water and a stirrup pump to dowse any fires that the bombing initiated. How on earth the authorities expected the fire-watchers to extinguish incendiary bombs, which the Germans used extensively, with a stirrup pump and a bucket of water, was never discussed. Obviously the real reason for the fire-watchers being there was to call the fire brigade should the factory sustain a direct hit and actually catch fire.

My parents lived in a rented house at 14, Frederick Road, but, owing to a quirky house numbering system and the fact that their house was situated at the forked junction with Victoria Road, my grandmother's house, despite being number 13, was a hundred yards down the road and on the opposite side. Nana's house, like my parents' house, was no different to any of the other three bed-roomed Victorian terraced houses that lined each side of the street and were occasionally interspersed with larger, four or five bed-roomed houses; evidence of a slightly more affluent past.

Growing up after the war was pretty straight forward, despite the food rationing and the generally difficult times that most people experienced as the country tried to recover from the devastation of the war and utter bankruptcy. As a child I didn't notice the hardship that my parents, like many others of their generation, endured because they shielded me from the more unpleasant problems. I never went hungry, lacked clothing or shoes, but I did know plenty of kids at school who were hungry, poorly clothed and wore what were commonly termed, 'Daily Mail boots' (given free to deserving families by that particular newspaper).

As the government struggled to improve the lot of ordinary people, so our family grew, with the appearance of my sister, Christine, in 1946, my brother, Michael, in 1948 and my brother, Peter, in 1950. We got along fairly well, but being the oldest boy by several years I tended to mix and play with similarly aged boys who lived close by rather than with my younger siblings.

We grew up in what could be termed a Christian household and we were taught Christian morals by our parents. My mother was the one who went to church regularly and she insisted that we should attend Sunday school when we were old enough. My only memories of that enforced attendance centred around the church organised street party after V.E. Day (Victory in Europe) in May 1945 (though I suspect it's the memories of the photographs of me attending that I actually recall, not the party itself because I was only three years old) and the Queen's coronation party in June 1953, at the little Baptist Church in Victoria Road, which I do remember. I found church-going all very boring and abandoned organised religion when I left school.

I attended Stechford Primary/Junior School and then, at the age of 11 or so, moved on to Bierton Road Secondary Modern School, having failed the eleven plus exam which would have probably given me access to a grammar school.

Bierton Road School catered for both boys and girls up to the age of 15, but was strictly segregated, there being no contact possible, even at break time. My secondary education was pretty mundane and not very interesting as far as I was concerned. I enjoyed history, science and metalwork, but not in any dedicated way.

Our form masters were mostly ex-military men who, after being demobbed in 1946 or so, had taken the government's two year teacher training course to enable them to re-establish themselves after the war. They were sticklers for discipline and used the cane frequently to keep order. We pupils were acutely aware that the last job these men had undertaken was killing the enemy and so we rarely messed around in their classes. Three of them remain in my memory, Mr Locke, the headmaster, of whom we saw very little, except at morning assembly, Mr Ryan and Mr Williams.

Mr Ryan was previously a warrant officer and stood at over six feet tall. His classes were conducted in absolute silence from us, unless we were requested to speak by him. His word was law and most sensible boys obeyed for fear of projectiles (usually a piece of chalk or a blackboard rubber) being thrown like hand grenades if he detected any mutinous mutterings whilst his back was turned as he wrote on the blackboard.

Mr Williams was a short, swarthy Welshman with large fleshy jowls, receding dark hair and glasses. I was never made aware of his previous military rank, but he also had a fetish for discipline. Every Monday morning before school he would stop at a nearby flower shop where they also sold flower pots, compost and such (there were no garden centres in those days), where he would buy a bamboo garden cane about three feet long. On entering the classroom he would sit behind his desk and take out his penknife (most men and boys carried a penknife in the 1950s) and split one end of the cane four ways for about six to eight inches along its length. To prevent the split from creeping, he applied some electrical insulating tape at the point where the splits ended. Meanwhile, we would sit in absolute silence while this work was being undertaken, knowing full well that at some time in the coming week we were bound to experience the results of his handiwork. The usual procedure was the swift application of three of the best to each palm should we say or do something he didn't think appropriate. Such was the usage of this cane that every Monday would see the need for a new one.

A bout of illness in 1954 saw me confined to my bed in our front room for a few months. My bed had been brought downstairs and placed in our bay window so that I could see what was going on in the street instead of having to stare at the four walls of my bedroom all day.

It was at this time that my mother encouraged me to take up basket weaving to pass the time. I must have made dozens of hanging baskets, flowerpot holders and shopping baskets, which, on my behalf, my mother sold to local people to recoup the cost of the materials. Eventually, however, I was sent to Kyre Park Hospital near Tenbury Wells, Worcester, because it was determined by our doctor that I was not improving at home. I had contracted what was described as a 'shadow' on one of my lungs (the early stages of Tuberculosis) and it took a good twelve months of bed rest at the hospital to clear up. Many of the young patients at Kyre Park were receiving the drug Streptomycin to cure their TB, luckily mine was not as aggressive and resting was considered a suitable cure.

The hospital was an isolated lovely old country house with huge grounds and it easily accommodated about 50 boys and girls up to the age of 14, strictly segregated of course. As our health slowly improved with all the bed rest or medicine, so the doctors would allow us time out of bed each day. It started with one hour and built up to four, and this enabled the more adventurous among us to explore the extensive wooded grounds and several lakes that surrounded the house. I was completely mesmerised by the tranquillity and beauty of the place and saw many wild creatures that I had only read about in books. My parents would visit me at the hospital as often as possible (about once a month), but it was a long way from Birmingham on the Midland Red bus and the fare was quite expensive because they often brought my siblings too.

I finally returned to school, having missed more than a full year, and tried to catch up, but it was a struggle. Accordingly, I had to contend with being placed in the 'B stream' for a while before moving back to the 'A stream' for my last year.

In early 1957, I was psyching myself up to leave school. However, having endured the useless interviews with the careers advice officer who could only suggest that I joined the Co-operative Wholesale Society as a delivery boy on their horse drawn bread and milk carts (a sure-fire dead-end job); I decided to look out for a job myself.

I had always been interested in railway engines (I spent my childhood watching them and recording their numbers over our back garden wall, which overlooked Stechford station, the main London to Birmingham line and the shunting yards) and therefore I considered joining the railways. However, I was also interested in cars and motorcycles (not that we could afford either one), so this avenue was also considered.

Having communicated these preferences to my parents, Dad made some enquiries and discovered that the railways were advertising for apprentice steam fitters at the Tyseley loco sheds (now the Birmingham Railway Museum). By some miracle my dad was able to arrange an interview at the loco sheds and we went there on the bus one Saturday morning. The foreman showed us round and I was fascinated by the huge locomotives that were in various stages of repair and immediately felt that this was the job for me. Dad was talking to the foreman, but I was more interested in looking at the huge connecting rods, pistons and wheel bearings that were being worked on or lying on the ground awaiting attention.

The next thing I knew, Dad had called me over to where he and the foreman were standing.

"Please tell the lad what you've just told me," said my dad, addressing the foreman.

I wondered what was coming next and looked at the foreman apprehensively.

"I was just telling your dad that steam locos are on their way out on the railways. They're all due to be replaced by diesel locomotives, so by the time you come out of your apprenticeship as a steam fitter, most of the steamers will have gone and you could be out of a job."

The look of disappointment on my face must have been obvious because he then said, "I know they are looking for apprentice mechanics at the Road Motor Engineers Department, situated next to number two loco shed at the Saltley Motive Power Department in Duddeston Mill Road."

Then, turning to my dad, he said, "The bloke you want is a Mr Lomas, he's the chief clerk there."

On the way home on the bus we discussed what the foreman had said and finally we both agreed that Dad should telephone Mr Lomas from the public phone box at Dad's works on the Monday, to see what was on offer and whether an interview could be arranged.

A few weeks later I found myself, along with both my parents, sitting in front of the chief clerk's desk in the main office at the Road Motor Engineers Department (RMED) in Duddeston Mill Road. I was reading through my indentured apprenticeship papers prior to signing them, having already survived the rigours of an initial interview and the medical check, much to my mother's relief.

She had been very annoyed with me over the medical check because, foolishly, I had celebrated my progress in the acquisition of a job thus far by drinking a half-pint of cider with some friends. We had persuaded an Irishman, who was standing around looking somewhat befuddled outside The Bull's Head pub in Station Road, to buy us a bottle of Bulmer's Cider at the 'Outdoor' (a retail shop selling alcohol and tobacco attached to the pub). As an incentive we had provided him with the appropriate amount of money and a single Wild Woodbine cigarette (a very popular brand manufactured by W.D & H.O Wills of Bristol).

When I returned home that evening, my mother, a very canny, strong willed Scotswoman, could smell the alcohol and she went ballistic, reminding me forcefully that I was due to have my medical examination the following morning at the railway health centre adjacent to New Street station in the city. She was convinced they would detect the alcohol in my body and, because I was under the legal drinking age, reject me as a candidate for employment as an apprentice. I went to bed that evening feeling very foolish and upset that I had caused so much trouble and worry for my mother and myself.

The ride into town on the bus with my mother the following morning was conducted in silence, my mother finding it very difficult to even look at me. Fortunately the examining doctor made no reference to alcohol whatsoever and, thinking about it later, I doubted there would be any residue in my body after only a half-pint of relatively weak cider and the passage of several hours. When the doctor gave me the all clear, my mother relented and cheered up a little. After another suitable and very heartfelt apology from me we went home on the bus, friends once again.

Having read through the document that would bind me to my employer, The British Transport Commission (British Railways, London Midland Region), for six years, I wondered what on earth I had let myself in for.

The main clauses read as follows:-

The British Transport Commission
(British Railways, London Midland Region)
Apprenticeship Agreement

Whereas:-
(A) The Commission are willing to accept the Apprentice to be taught and instructed in the craft of Motor Fitter.

(B) The Guardian having enquired into the nature of the business conducted by the Commission desires that the Apprentice shall learn the craft of Motor Fitter in the service of the Commission.

Now it is hereby agreed as follows:-

(1) The Apprentice, of his own free will and the consent of the Guardian, hereby binds himself as an apprentice to the Commission in the craft of Motor Fitter on conditions hereinafter appearing.

(2) The Commission hereby agrees with the Guardian and the Apprentice:-

> (a) That the Commission will accept the Apprentice as an apprentice of the Commission from the 15th day of April 1957 to the 15th day of April 1963.
>
> (b) That the Commission will arrange, through its officers and assistants during the said term for the Apprentice to be taught and instructed in the craft of Motor Fitter.
>
> (c) That the Commission will pay to the Apprentice during the said term and so long as he shall be able to and does actually perform his service, wages at the rate prescribed from time to time for apprentices in the service of the Commission.
>
> (d) That the Commission will grant reasonable facilities to the Apprentice for attendance at classes in courses approved by them, subject always to satisfactory progress having been made by the Apprentice and providing his progress remains satisfactory.
>
> (e) That the Commission will refund to the Apprentice fees paid for all classes attended with their approval, subject always to eighty per cent of possible attendance being made, to satisfactory conduct at all times by the Apprentice and to the taking of appropriate examinations.

(f) That on satisfactory completion of the apprenticeship the Certificate attached to this Agreement shall be completed by the Commission and the Agreement shall then become the property of the Apprentice.

(3) The Guardian hereby agrees with the Commission:-

(a) That he will provide for the material needs of the Apprentice during the term of the apprenticeship.

(b) That he will, to the best of his ability, restrain the Apprentice from all harmful influences during the said apprenticeship.

(4) The Apprentice and the Guardian as surety for the Apprentice hereby jointly and severally agree with the Commission:-

(a) That the Apprentice shall during the whole of the said term honestly and faithfully serve the Commission and diligently apply himself to the learning of the craft aforesaid.

(b) That he shall keep the Commission's secrets and obey all lawful and reasonable commands and requirements of the Commission and its authorised representatives.

(c) That he shall not absent himself during the usual working hours without the consent of the Commission.

(d) That the Apprentice shall not during the said apprenticeship engage in any other occupation or business whatsoever which might interfere with the successful carrying out of his apprenticeship.

(e) That the Apprentice shall attend and diligently study at such evening classes and day classes as may from time to time be approved by the Commission.

(f) That the Apprentice shall upon request of the Commission apply to the proper authority for and produce for inspection such certificates of attendance, reports or results of examinations as may be required.

(5) If the Apprentice shall at any time be guilty of any breach or non-observance of any of the covenants herein provided or of any gross misconduct the Commission may forthwith discharge him and this Agreement shall thereupon be cancelled.

The chief clerk looked at me and began to explain that I would be working a 44 hour week, 8am to 5pm every weekday, with half an hour for lunch and two tea breaks of 15 minutes at 10am and 3pm. In those days, Saturday was just part of the working week and I would be required to work from 8am to midday to complete the 44 hours required.

Mr Lomas then withdrew a sheet of paper from the top drawer of his desk and handed it to me. It laid out the pay rates for the various years of my apprenticeship. A quick glance confirmed that in my first year I would be paid the princely sum of £1-10 shillings (£1.50) per week (£34 at 2016 values) and in my last year the pay would be £7-10 shillings (£7.50) per week (£149 at 2016 values) plus any increases agreed nationally during the period of my apprenticeship.

I can assure the reader that the subsequent pay increases agreed nationally were pitifully small and amounted to no more than a few shillings per week.

The chief clerk then quickly ran through some other details regarding welfare, union membership and safety requirements before inviting my father to read the apprenticeship agreement. A few minutes later my dad passed the document back to the chief clerk who, after signing it, pushed it back towards my dad who also signed and passed it to me. I looked at the two signatures for just a moment and then signed across a tuppenny-ha'penny (1p) postage stamp that had been affixed by Mr Lomas to make the whole thing legal.

The agreement was now signed, sealed and delivered. I would, in three days' time, be an apprentice in the employ of the British Transport Commission (British Railways, London Midland Region) who would train me to be a motor fitter (motor mechanic) over a period of six years; job done and dusted.

For those readers unfamiliar with pre-1971 UK currency, all you have to remember is that there were 12 pennies (d) to the shilling and 20 shillings (s) to the pound. Therefore, there were 240 'old' pennies (d) to the pound. When decimalisation came in, the pound was divided into 100 'new' pennies (p), resulting in one new penny being worth 2.4 old pennies. Obviously a certain amount of rounding was required with certain values in order to reach sensible conversions between the two. To keep the rounding to a minimum and prevent price inflation, the government introduced a new half-penny coin, which was equivalent to 1.2 old pennies. It was withdrawn in 1984.

For those readers unfamiliar with the Imperial system of measurement, suffice it to say that one foot is equivalent to about 300 millimetres, a mile is approximately 1.6 kilometres and a gallon is about 4.5 litres.

Chapter 2
MY FIRST DAY

Not only was Monday the 15th April 1957 my first day at work, it was also my 15th birthday. I had left school during the Easter break and now I was legally entitled to work.

I woke early and prepared myself for the adventure yet to come. Mother had made me some breakfast, as usual, and I ate it quickly as I sat there at the kitchen table wondering what was in store for me. She wished me a happy birthday and said, "Don't forget to look out for Mr Ellerman on the station. He said he would accompany you to the workshop."

I nodded and drained the tea from my second cup that morning. Mr Ellerman or Ernest, as he was known to my parents, was the senior driver at the RMED and lived in one of the railway cottages on Station Road with his wife and family. He had known my parents for quite a while and so it was natural that he should offer to help, especially since we were both going to the same place that morning.

My mother handed me a pack of sandwiches and a thermos flask of tea, which I placed in my new haversack, purchased from the army surplus stores in town on Saturday morning. I had also purchased a pair of ex-army boots from the same place just a week before and had worn the boots on several occasions to break them in. Feeling the tightness of these new boots on my feet, I hoped they would be pliable enough not to give me blisters through the long day ahead.

I said goodbye to my mother and my siblings, who were singing *Happy Birthday* at the top of their voices, walked through the hall to the front door and down the front path. Turning left in the street, I made my way to the entrance of Stechford railway station, about 100 yards away. In those days this wooden Victorian building was situated on Station Road, but after a fire in the late 1960s, they demolished the charred remains and replaced it with a smaller, modern station with an entrance on Frederick Road. I bought a return ticket to Adderley Park, which was just one stop from Stechford in the direction of the city. I think it cost around one shilling (5p), but it may have been even cheaper.

The original Stechford station was built high on the road bridge across the main London to Birmingham railway lines, so there was a long, steep set of steps which led to the platforms below. As I negotiated the steps, I saw the unmistakable form of Mr Ellerman on the platform. He was a big man, six feet tall at least, and quite large around the girth too. He resembled those illustrations of 'The Laughing Policeman' of music hall fame, especially since he wore a smart black railway driver's uniform and a peaked cap. He greeted me cordially and we continued the small talk until the train arrived, at which time we bundled ourselves into a single compartment, along with several other people, and remained silent until Adderley Park. On alighting from the train and negotiating the steep steps up to Bordesley Green Road, Mr Ellerman began to tell me about some of the foremen and other notable characters who also worked at the RMED.

At the top of the station steps we turned right and walked past the Morris Commercial factory and crossed Arden Road into Ash Road. At the end of Ash Road, at the bottom of the hill, we crossed Adderley Road into Duddeston Mill Road. The distance from the station was approximately five-eighths of a mile, a reasonably easy walk after a hard day's work, I thought. On the left hand side of Duddeston Mill Road was a long high wall, solidly built from blue engineering bricks. About a quarter of the way along its length was a pair of large wooden sliding doors with a small wicket gate set into the left hand section.

"In you go, lad," said Mr Ellerman, pointing at the wicket gate.

Beyond the gate was a very tiny yard area which sloped up to another pair of wooden sliding doors that also sported a wicket gate. Upon passing through it, I found myself looking at a large workshop.

So this was the Road Motor Engineers Department of British Railways, London Midland Region, eh?

I was impressed.

We turned right, walked along a gangway between some inspection pits and a number of smaller workshops, which were separated from the main workshop by weld-mesh wire, until we came to the end wall where the time clock was situated. Mr Ellerman clocked on and advised me to wait near the clock for the general foreman to arrive. It was just gone half past seven, so I had at least 25 minutes to kill. Whilst I was waiting, three other young lads of about my age turned up and also waited awkwardly near the time clock.

"Are you a new apprentice?" said one of them, pointing at me.

"Yes, are you three new apprentices too?" I replied.

They nodded silently.

"All right, you four lads come down here and get your clock cards."

The balding middle-aged man wearing a clean blue boiler suit was standing in the entrance to a small office situated next to the weld-mesh separated workshops that looked like large 'cages'. We all obeyed immediately and walked towards the office. He called our names in turn and handed us a clock card each.

"Go and clock on now and remember to do it every morning and to clock off every evening when you finish, otherwise you won't get paid. There is a number on your card to coincide with a number on the racks on each side of the clock. Don't put your cards in the wrong slots, do you understand?"

We nodded apprehensively and walked back to the clock clutching our cards. The area was now beginning to get crowded, with men arriving singly or in groups, clocking on and changing into their overalls next to the individual lockers that lined the wall on each side of the clock.

Observing the clocking on procedure for a few minutes, we realised that it entailed putting the clock card into a slot under the clock face and moving a large lever, which was situated at the side of the clock, sharply downwards. This action produced a single chime from a bell inside the clock, thus indicating the success of the operation. One of the new lads moved forward and clocked on quite easily, soon to be followed by the rest of us. We placed our cards in the correct slots on the racks and wondered what was going to happen next.

The man in the clean boiler suit called us to his office again and said, "Have you clocked on properly?"

We nodded in unison.

He then said, "Right, I'm Sid Bartlett, the foreman of the repair shop. This bit here," waving his arm around to indicate the area he was talking about.

"The general foreman, Mr Goodman, will be here any minute and he will tell you what to do next, so go and wait by the clock again."

We dutifully shuffled out of the foreman's small office, walked back to the clock and stood in a small group watching the other men clocking on and saying good morning when similarly greeted by them. We then took the opportunity of introducing ourselves and telling each other from which part of the city we hailed. After a few minutes we ran out of conversation, so we stood silently waiting for Mr Goodman.

Suddenly, a tall, balding man with the remnants of ginger hair around the sides and back of his head and dressed in a brown cowgown (a Midland term for a long, brown coloured coat-like overall similar to a doctor's white coat), walked across from the other side of the huge workshop and pointed at us.

"Right you lads, gather round. Have you clocked on?" he enquired in a mild, but noticeable, Cockney accent.

We all nodded.

"Good, follow me and I will show you around and then I shall decide who goes where."

The total workshop was about 250 feet long by 200 feet wide, with a roof supporting wall, which had several large access arches, separating it into two distinct, but unequally sized areas. Viewed from the Duddeston Mill Road entrance, the smaller overhaul shop, including a small machine shop and diesel pump overhaul shop, was to the left. The larger repair shop, including the four inspection pits and the stores beyond, was to the right. On the opposite side from the Duddeston entrance was the carpenter's shop and two paint shops. On the same side as the Duddeston entrance, but opposite the inspection pits, were the specialist repair cages and the repair shop foreman's office. The specialist repair cages included a radiator repair cage, an electrician's cage, a battery charging and overhaul cage, a tyre repair cage and a welding cage. On the adjacent end wall to the right was the door to the lavatories and washing facilities, the time clock, the stores issue counter, numerous individual lockers and the entrance to the stores and administrative offices that occupied the first floor above the stores. Further along this wall was the main vehicular entrance, capable of accommodating all sizes of trucks, buses and mobile cranes.

The general foreman's office was situated between the two main workshops in the middle arch of the dividing wall and was set high so that he had an uninterrupted view of the whole workshop area. About 20 feet above was the massive roof of the repair workshop. It was of the 'sawtooth' design and made entirely of wire-reinforced glass panels set into steel frames, which allowed a surprising amount of light into the whole area. Far from being a 'Dark Satanic Mill', the repair workshop was pleasant, airy and full of light.

Because the overhaul workshop had an electrically operated five ton overhead crane, which was able to traverse the whole length and width of the workshop, the roof there had fewer glass panels. However, there were very large windows in the wall opposite that allowed more light into the area, so it was only marginally darker than the repair workshop. Included in the overhaul section of the workshop was a small machine shop equipped with a radial driller, a shaping machine, two lathes, a cylinder boring and honing machine and various other small machine tools. Also included in the overhaul shop was an enclosed 'clean room' for the repair of diesel pumps and injectors. Mr Goodman, we learnt, was in overall charge of both workshops, but he had four foremen or chargehands looking after the overhaul shop, the repair shop, the paint shop and the carpenter's shop.

All in all the RMED workshops at Saltley were well equipped to carry out all the work required to keep the huge fleet of railway road vehicles that operated in the Midland Region in good mechanical condition. The most numerous of these vehicles being the three-wheeled Scammell Scarab tractor units of three and six ton capacity, together with thousands of flat-bed or van-bodied trailers, also of three and six ton capacity, with wooden platforms.

Of course, Saltley wasn't the only repair centre, there were satellite workshops dotted all around the city and the region, but Saltley was the main workshop where all the major overhaul work was carried out.

After being shown around and meeting the various foremen and chargehands, Mr Goodman sat us down in his office and told us how our apprenticeships would develop.

He explained that the first thing required of us was to recognise the names of the various tools and equipment we would be using and to understand what the myriad parts that make up a vehicle were called and their function. Consequently, all four of us were to be assigned to the stores for three months. In the stores, Mr Goodman explained, we would quickly become familiar with the names of the various parts and tools. After serving our allotted time in the stores, he told us that we would be placed in the various cages to learn how to repair and overhaul the bits and pieces that make up a vehicle. Later, we would be sent to the machine shop. Only when we had completed that part of our training could we be assigned to a fitter for general repair work, engine overhaul or transmission/axle overhaul. He also explained that because there were four of us starting all on the same day, he could not guarantee in what order our assignments would occur, but would do his best to see that we did things in the right order. He then added that since there was plenty of work to do in the stores, it didn't matter that all four of us were to begin our training there.

"Right, you lot, follow me to the stores to meet the senior storekeeper."

The stores department was a dark, dingy place with barely any natural light, so the dozens of feeble electric light bulbs hanging from the ceiling had to be kept on all day. The place stank of oil and kerosene and was dusty, very dusty.

We followed Mr Goodman into the depths of the stores to where there was a small glass-panelled office where two elderly men sat at a long bench-like desk sorting through thousands of postcard-sized stock cards. Mr Goodman opened the door of the office and said, "These are the new lads, Mr Shook."

Mr Shook stood up and ventured to the door of his office, while the other chap in there remained seated, but turned to look at us and smile.

"Right, you will all be working here for three months, so behave yourselves, all right?" said Mr Shook in a broad Birmingham accent.

He, like most of the foremen and chargehands, wore a brown cow-gown, but this one was long enough to almost touch his shoes. The reason for this was that Mr Shook was only about five feet tall. He may have been shorter, but he was certainly a head below me and I had not yet grown to my eventual five feet, ten inches. He had on a pair of thick horn rimed glasses and was bald from front to back apart from a small fringe of black hair at the sides of his head. He reminded me of the comedian and variety performer, Max Wall, such was the uncanny facial resemblance.

Mr Shook then called out the name 'Jock' and moments later a short, thickset man wearing a brown cow-gown appeared from behind some shelving, muttering incoherently twelve to the dozen.

"This is Jock; take your orders from him, all right?" said Mr Shook, as he dived back into his office.

Mr Goodman left us to it and we all looked over at Jock who smiled before saying something quite unintelligible, his Glaswegian accent obliterating all understanding as his words peppered us with the rapidity of a machine gun. We spent the rest of the morning trying to understand Jock and take in the things he was showing us.

He waxed lyrical (at least I think he did) over such places as the oil and kerosene store, the cotton waste store, the acid carboy store and the hundreds of feet of shelving which contained all the spare parts for the hundreds of different makes and models of vehicles owned by the railways.

At lunch time we sat with Jock behind the stores issue counter eating our sandwiches, still trying to interpret his words. Happily, towards the end of the day, I became more used to Jock's accent and was able to understand most of what he said.

In the afternoon a clerk from the general office above the stores (Jock called it the 'Holy of Holies') came to see us clutching two workman's train passes in his hand. He handed one to me and the remaining pass to one of the other lads. What a pleasant surprise, now it was possible for me to travel to and from work on the train at a 75% discount, thus saving me something like four shillings and sixpence (approximately 22p) per week. The reader might think that it was not much to get excited about, but when earning only 30 shillings (£1.50) a week and retaining ten shillings (50p) for myself before handing the rest to my mother, it was an absolute fortune. Because they didn't live convenient to a railway station, the other two lads could not use the train to get to work, which must have been something of a disappointment for them, I'm sure.

Later, just before clocking off time, the foreman carpenter came over to the stores issue counter, saw me standing behind it and said, "Come on, lad, we've been waiting to measure you for your overalls."

We had been issued with temporary overalls earlier in the morning, but they were pretty ragged things and didn't fit very well, so I eagerly followed the foreman chippie across the workshop to the carpenter's area in the far corner of the overhaul shop. The other three lads were told to wait in the stores until it was their turn.

"Right, stand upright against this plank so that I can mark how tall you are in pencil," said the foreman chippie.

I did as I was told and stood upright with my head touching the plank at the back. No sooner had I assumed this position, than there was an almighty bang and my head went forward under the force of a hammer blow to the plank directly behind my head. It hurt like hell and I shouted out, but all the chippies thought it was hilarious and roared with laughter, including the foreman.

I rubbed the back of my head and said, "What was that for?"

"That's your initiation to the workshop, lad, everyone has to go through it."

"Well, it's not very funny and it hurts," I said, trying not to be too assertive.

"Oh, stop your moaning, it's only a joke," said the foreman.

"Now stay here while I fetch another lad for the same treatment."

They 'did' all four of us and would not allow those of us who had been 'done' to say a word to those awaiting their initiation.

Ten minutes later, feeling somewhat hurt and a bit foolish, we clocked off and made our separate ways home, hoping that what had happened in the carpenter's shop was the first and the last of the initiation ceremonies to be conducted on new apprentices.

Several months later, a young apprentice was knocked semi-unconscious and had to attend the hospital because of this stupid activity by the chippies. Thereafter, this particular initiation ceremony was quietly discontinued.

At home, after our evening meal, I told my family all about my first day at work, remembering to omit the stupid business of the plank and the hammer. Later, my mother produced a home-made birthday cake, which we all shared and the whole family wished me happy birthday once again.

Chapter 3
THE BRITISH RAILWAYS ROAD VEHICLE FLEET

During the 1950s and 60s, British Railways ran one of the largest fleets of road vehicles in the country and purchased something like 600 to 900 new ones every year to replace those that were scrapped at the end of their useful life. However, as the years rolled by, the number of new vehicles being purchased reduced dramatically, due entirely to the never ending financial troubles of the organisation. Similarly, the scrappage rate increased, especially after 1961, thus the fleet slowly declined.

When I joined the railways in 1957, they had a total fleet of 15,359 vehicles, of which 10,680 were tractor units and 4,679 were rigid vehicles. Of the 10,680 tractor units, the majority (probably about 60%) were three-wheeled Scammell Scarabs. They were of three and six ton capacity, designed in 1948 and used for pulling trailers. The older version of the Scarab, the Scammell Mechanical Horse (MH3 and MH6), also of three and six ton capacity and designed in 1934, were slowly being phased out. These Scammell products were very versatile and well suited to goods yard operations and crowded town traffic conditions because they were exceptionally manoeuvrable. Even with a trailer attached they were able to turn through 360 degrees well within a circle 20 feet in diameter. The other vehicle that figured quite prominently in the tractor unit category was the Karrier Bantam, a four-wheeled unit and therefore less manoeuvrable than the Scarab.

In 1963, when I had finished my apprenticeship, the total fleet had declined to 13,200 vehicles, of which 9,240 were tractor units and 3,960 were rigid vehicles. This represented an overall shrinkage in the fleet of some 14% since 1957. When I finally left the employ of the railways in 1965, the total fleet had declined sharply to 11,700 vehicles of which 8,250 were tractor units and 3,450 were rigid vehicles. In only eight years almost a quarter of the fleet had disappeared.

These reductions increased dramatically after 1963, due to the plan (*The Reshaping of British Railways*) produced by Dr Richard Beeching in that year, in which he recommended ripping up 6,000 miles of railway track, the closure of 2,363 stations and the culling of over 70,000 railway jobs. The government accepted the plan and the cuts began almost immediately. This decimation of the railways affected everything, including the RMED. In 1965, the writing was clearly on the wall and many people at that time, me included, began looking for more secure futures.

During the same period the number of flat-bed and van-type trailers had declined from 35,000 in 1957 to 31,500 in 1963. When I left the railways in 1965, their number stood at 28,000.

Of course, not all these vehicles were serviced and repaired in Birmingham, since they were distributed very unevenly throughout British Railways' six regions. However, bearing in mind the importance of Birmingham and the Black Country as industrial centres at that time, it is reasonable to assume that there would have been a fair proportion of railway road vehicles in our area.

My best guess is that the Road Motor Engineers Department at Saltley, together with all the small district workshops in the city, maintained and overhauled something like 25% of the total fleet of vehicles and trailers. In 1957, that would mean somewhere in the region of 3,800 vehicles and 8,750 trailers.

THE NEXT TWENTY-ONE MONTHS
(April 1957 to January 1959)

Whilst I was embarking on my journey through the world of work, there were other things going on in the country and elsewhere to worry and ponder about. To put things into perspective, here's a sample of the headlines from those 21 months.

April 1957
Government says National Service to end in 1960.

December 1957
Train crash at Lewisham kills 90.

February 1958
Plane carrying Manchester United team crashes at Munich.

January 1959
Racing ace, Mike Hawthorn, killed in private car crash.

I can't remember the actual order in which I served my three months in each of the various cages and my six months in the machine shop, so I have simply listed the cages in the order that they were situated along the wall from the repair shop foreman's office to the Duddeston entrance doors. The machine shop was to the left of these entrance doors, on the other side of the dividing wall in the overhaul shop. I have also recorded various incidents and milestones that were relevant at the time. All dates refer to the middle of the month since I started work on the 15th.

Since all four of us new apprentices began our training in the stores, it's logical to begin my story there.

Chapter 4
THE STORES (THE GLORY HOLE)
April 1957 to July 1957

As I have mentioned, Mr Shook was the stores foreman, but we hardly ever saw him, except through the windows of his office where he spent all his time sifting and sorting through stock cards. He was not a very sociable man and left us in the care of Jock, who was the stores issue clerk. The other man in Mr Shook's office was Ted, a jolly little man, very happy to share jokes and anecdotes with all the stores staff, including us apprentices, but he too seemed to spend most of his time sifting through stock cards.

At the back of the stores was the goods inwards and stores loading bay. Here trucks were received with all sorts of spare parts and equipment or loaded to deliver material to the district workshops. The loading bay was overseen by a rather grumpy middle-aged man, but for the life of me I can't remember his name. We apprentices were discouraged from going anywhere near this loading bay, especially when the chap was actually receiving material. We learnt from Jock that the man was terrified we might steal something before it had been checked in and that he would be blamed. We apprentices thought this a very odd attitude to take, so it was little wonder that we avoided him most of the time.

Since there were four of us in the stores at the same time we shared what work there was to do, though in truth it was not overly physical or onerous. In fact, much of the time we were bored stiff and resorted to wandering through the stores looking at the various bits and pieces, trying to work out what they were.

Having now become used to Jock's really thick Glaswegian accent, we began to learn more about him. He had been in the Black Watch regiment during the war and, despite being in a strictly reserved occupation (I believe he was a shipwright before the war), he had volunteered. Making it clear to his employer that he wanted to do his bit, he simply ignored their protestations and went off and joined up, regardless. He had been wounded in North Africa fighting against Rommel's Afrika Korps, which left him with a gammy leg. He showed us the old wound one day and I was amazed by how much flesh had been gouged out of his calf. The wound had healed all right, but it left Jock with a weak leg and a distinct limp.

He was very patient with us in the first few weeks, but as soon as he thought we should be able to deal with things ourselves, he more or less left us to it.

The job primarily consisted of standing by the stores issue counter waiting for the fitters and other apprentices to present requisitions for parts and tools.

The paper requisitions were completed in Mr Goodman's office by a middle-aged lady clerk called Heather. She was the darling of the workshop and always looked very presentable, despite the light blue bib and braces overalls and the highly coloured headscarf she wore every day. Heather was always extremely pleasant and helpful and also happened to be a Scot.

It was Heather who handed out our wage packets on Friday mornings; all carefully placed in name order inside a shoebox-sized shallow wooden tray.

She always smiled and usually commented in her lilting Highland accent, "Here's your hard earned wages, Kenneth. Don't spend the money all at once, now."

If you were out of the workshop when Heather did her wages round, you had to go to the chief accountant in the main office upstairs to collect your money, but he wasn't half as good-looking or as pleasant as Heather.

After Heather had written out the requisition, it was signed by Mr Goodman and then by the foreman or chargehand of whichever department the person presenting it was assigned. My job was to check that the requisition had been signed by both parties and then note the part number and location of the part, which Heather had specified on the requisition. Having done all that, I would then go into the depths of the stores to retrieve the part from the appropriate bin. Naturally, there were occasions when the bin location was incorrectly stated or the part had been placed in the wrong bin. I would then have to go searching or recheck the location against the part number in the file index in Mr Shook's office. Most of the time Mr Shook, having simply looked at the part number, could tell me the location from memory; quite an achievement in a store that must have held thousands of individual parts. While all this was going on, the chap who had proffered the requisition would become impatient waiting at the counter and start shouting my name and suggesting that I had fallen asleep.

"Come on you daft bugger, I ain't got all day you know," was a frequent comment.

Once the part had been handed to the person requesting it, he was required to sign the requisition to complete the procedure. I then placed the requisition in a wooden box which Mr Shook or Ted collected each evening to enable them to reconcile the stock the following morning and order more if necessary.

I was also required to serve loose oil and kerosene, tapped from barrels at the back of the stores. On one or two occasions the huge two gallon measures would slip from my grip and the contents would end up all over the floor, much to everyone's dismay and annoyance.

Naturally the mickey-taking continued for a few weeks and all four of us apprentices, at one time or another, were sent off to the receiving bay to find the long weight, the left-handed screwdriver or the skyhooks. The long weight entailed going to ask the grumpy man at the receiving bay if he would kindly supply this long weight, since it was urgently required in the overhaul shop. He would then indicate that I would have to wait. Well, after about five minutes it suddenly dawned on me what it was all about, 'weight – wait', how very amusing. As soon as I realised this, I warned my fellow apprentices and that put the kibosh on that little piece of nonsense until they thought up some other ways of humiliating us.

During our time in the stores we were measured properly for our free issue of three pairs of overalls; one pair on, one in the wash and one spare, just in case. The whole scheme was run by a British Railways owned industrial laundry service somewhere in the city and the clean overalls were delivered weekly by a man in a van. We were also given the opportunity of buying some toe protector boots, which we all did and they took the money from our wages at the rate of a single shilling (5p) per week.

The four of us were delighted when Mr Goodman came to the stores to provide us with some good news. We were absolutely thrilled to learn that we were entitled to three, absolutely free, second class return rail passes to any destination within mainland Britain every year, plus as many 'quarter fare' warrants that we wanted. This was quite a perk, of which everyone made good use. Who wouldn't?

At the end of our three months, all four of us new apprentices were quite proficient in providing what everyone wanted from the stores and we realised that Mr Goodman had been right. The experience had taught us about tools and equipment and the names and function of the thousands of spare parts that fitted every conceivable vehicle on the fleet. As the four of us left the stores to go to our respective assignments in the cages, we realised that we now had more knowledge of motor vehicles and tools that when we had started, and that must have been a good thing.

Chapter 5
MAKING FRIENDS AND ENEMIES

Working in the stores enabled me to meet almost every person working at the RMED, including all of the other apprentices. I got on well with almost everyone, but there were a few exceptions. I never really forgave the foreman chippie over the measuring incident and he didn't help himself much either, since he always had something rude or disparaging to say about 'techie' apprentices, as he called us. Apparently the carpenter's shop used to take apprentices, but since the amount of wood used in the construction of motor vehicles was becoming negligible, the management decided to discontinue carpentry apprentices. Only the old Mechanical Horses had wooden cabs and they were disappearing fast. The Scarab still had wooden floorboards, as did some of the other older vehicles, but the main occupation of the chippie's shop, as far as I could see, was the renewal of the wooden planks in the thousands of flat-bed trailers that littered every goods yard in the city. They also renewed the fibreglass front cowlings on the Scarabs too. I think the foreman chippie was somewhat peeved over this downgrading of his importance and took his frustrations out on us whenever possible, with snide remarks and downright belligerence if we ever had to approach him for any reason.

There was a much older apprentice who was a bit of a pain in the neck too. He was probably around 20 years old and, having seen it all, he tended to deride and sneer at anything we younger apprentices had to say. It was unusual for an apprentice of his age to be still working in the main workshop, because he should have been serving some time in the district workshops dotted around the city and the region. He was a bully, unbelievably obnoxious and lazy. I doubt any one of the younger apprentices liked him. I certainly didn't because he would always take the opportunity to clip you around the back of the head if he passed you by and would push in at the stores counter if there were other younger boys there. He had been the one wielding the hammer during the overall measuring prank too. He was a tall, well built youth, tending towards being fat. Nonetheless, he was quite capable of flattening us younger lads and threatened to do so quite often and for no apparent reason. I suspected that he had been retained at the central workshops so that he could be observed by senior management. My theory was more or less proved several months later when we heard that he had 'left the job'. This was most unusual for an apprentice just about to finish his time.

There was an apprentice who had joined a few weeks before me. His name was Frank Moore and he lived with his parents in Bowyer Road, not far from the workshop. He was a bit of a card, always joking and larking about and over the months he came to be a good friend, along with another lad called Malcolm Simper, who lived in Tamworth. Those friendships lasted until we had all finished our time and beyond. Sadly we all lost touch with each other when Frank went off to join the air force and I left the railways in 1965.

All in all I got on well with most of the people who worked at the main workshops and even though they sometimes took the mickey and played pranks, no real harm was ever done or meant to be done. We younger apprentices were seeing the world of work for what it was and we were definitely beginning to grow out of our schoolboy ways.

Notwithstanding the so-called grown up ways of the workplace, many of us younger boys were somewhat surprised to discover that some people in the workshop had nicknames. We thought that sort of thing only happened in the school playground. I can't remember all of them now, but I do recall that Mr Goodman was always referred to as 'Benny' after the famous American bandleader and song writer, Benny Goodman. When the film staring Charlton Heston was released in 1961, the lads in the workshop immediately dubbed Sid Bartlett, the repair shop foreman, as 'El Cid'. It should be noted by the reader, however, that anyone who could have been more unlike Charlton Heston than Sid Bartlett, would be really difficult to find. Obviously these nicknames were only used when we knew both foremen were well out of earshot.

Chapter 6
THE RADIATOR CAGE (THE RAD CAGE)
July 1957 to October 1957

The rad cage, as it was called, was right next to Sid Bartlett's office and was about 20 feet long and 15 feet wide. The man in charge was called Freddy and he could have been in his late 50s, early 60s, it was very difficult to tell. He wore the usual blue boiler suit and a flat cap which, according to popular rumour, he was never seen to be without, even when he was at home indoors. He smoked Woodbine cigarettes almost continuously, so much so that his index and second fingers of his right hand were stained a really dark brown with nicotine. Freddy was a Brummie boy through and through and spoke with a very pronounced Brummie accent. It was also rumoured that he used to be quite rough and tough as a young man and was a member of one of the infamous Birmingham street gangs of the early 1900s, generally known as the Peaky Blinders. Certainly his distinct lack of several front teeth would support a violent and shady past. Now though he was a pleasant old chap who would address everyone, including the foremen, as, 'our kid'.

"Oweyaumagooin, ah kid?" was his usual greeting in the morning.

For the uninitiated, "How are you going, our kid?"

My job in the rad cage was to help Freddy overhaul, repair and pressure test radiators removed from vehicles that came in for overhaul. We had a stock of various repaired radiators and operated a sort of part-exchange scheme for the main workshop and the district workshops. They brought a damaged radiator in and we gave them a reconditioned one in exchange.

We were also, for some reason lost in the passage of time, responsible for the maintenance and repair of the large Weaver steam cleaning plant, which was located in the front yard, opposite the entrance to the number two loco shed. It was here that almost everything was steam cleaned prior to being worked on in the service and repair workshop or the overhaul workshop.

Many of the heavy-duty truck radiators, such as those manufactured by Scammell, were capable of being dismantled and the various parts renewed because the top and bottom tanks were bolted to the cooling core with rubber gaskets in between. The individual core cooling tubes were held in place by rubber seals, which could also be renewed when they leaked. Cheaper radiators were soldered or brazed together, but we could still unbutton them, make repairs and re-solder or re-braze them back together again.

Pressure testing radiators involved placing an expandable rubber bung into the hose outlet in the bottom tank, filling the radiator with cold water and then introducing another bung, which had an airline fitting through the middle of it, to the top hose outlet. Once the bungs were tight and there were no obvious leaks, the workshop's airline hose, which delivered compressed air at 100 pounds per square inch, was attached to the fitting in the top bung and turned on. If the radiator could withstand five minutes at this pressure it was declared fit for service and placed in our stock or returned to the vehicle from whence it came.

Inevitably we had our failures, with either the bungs being blown out or the radiator splitting under pressure. As you can imagine, it was always inattentive apprentices not tightening the expanding bungs properly who caused most of the failures. When one of the bungs shot out under pressure of the compressed air, the water inside the radiator spurted out too, soaking everyone around. Freddy would curse and swear like a trooper every time it happened and everyone working nearby would cheer. On the few occasions it happened to me, both Freddy and I got absolutely soaked and had go to our lockers near the time clock to change into dry overalls. On these occasions Sid Bartlett would come out of his office as we were changing and say, "I see you've been lumbered with yet another dozy bleeder then, Freddy."

Though Freddy cursed us apprentices to hell and back if he got wet, he never held a grudge no matter how many times it happened. He was very kind like that and spent a great deal of his time teaching me, and no doubt scores of other apprentices, how to solder, braze and remove dents from top and bottom tanks very quickly and proficiently. My time spent in the rad cage and Freddy's expert tutoring added yet more knowledge and another set of skills to my repertoire.

Chapter 7
THE ELECTRICIAN'S/BATTERY CAGE
(THE SPARKY'S CAGE)
October 1957 to January 1958

The electrician's cage was the largest of all the cages with four people working in there. The man in charge was a somewhat overbearing Black Country man of about 60 years of age, whose name, I seem to remember, was Bill. He was a mountain of a man and suffered terribly from a back injury, which had apparently been inflicted during his time as a professional football player in his youth. To support his back and to relieve the pain that he must have suffered all day long, he wore a thick leather corset underneath his blue cow-gown, but on the outside of his shirt and trousers. It extended from under his arms right down to his hips. As a result of wearing this leather armour, he creaked and squeaked loudly every time he moved as the shiny leather rubbed against itself where it overlapped. Bill walked with great difficulty using two sticks and his gait was as rolling as a sailor's in a storm. He was not a very happy man and probably had little time for apprentices.

Bill's job, in addition to supervising the others in the cage, was the overhaul of starter motors, dynamos and magnetos. One of the other chaps was responsible for testing the units that Bill had reconditioned, and he had a special test rig designed for the job. The third man in the sparky's cage was a general automotive electrician named Frank, who responded to requests from the fitters to repair wiring and other electrical problems on actual vehicles, so he spent most of his day out in the main workshop.

The remaining employee was a labourer who cleaned the component parts of the various units after they had been stripped out. He also looked after the battery cage next door, where batteries were charged, re-plated and generally refurbished. As with the rad cage, the sparky's cage operated an exchange scheme for all the electrical equipment and batteries they overhauled.

The usual pattern for an apprentice was to spend a month with Bill to learn about the intricacies of overhauling starter motors, dynamos and magnetos. Then a couple of weeks with the bloke who tested them and a couple of weeks with the battery man. The remaining month was spent with Frank, to become familiar with repairing electrical faults on vehicles themselves.

Because all the apprentices were destined to become fitters (mechanics), it was not deemed necessary to secure a deep working knowledge of vehicle electrics. However, electrical fault diagnoses on vehicles could be difficult and some additional time, say another month, spent with Frank would have been ideal in my view.

My month with Bill was nothing short of purgatory. Only occasionally would he allow an apprentice to actually overhaul a piece of electrical equipment, and thus it was with me. Consequently, my days were, more often than not, spent standing at his side watching his every move and answering the daft questions he had a habit of throwing at you when he thought your attention had waned.

"Why can't you boil an egg on top of a mountain?" was one of his favourites, which would always be delivered loudly in his broad Black Country accent.

As a result of this boredom during my time with Bill, I would occasionally wander off for an hour or so to speak to other apprentices and watch what they were up to in the repair shop or the overhaul shop. This would annoy Bill, consequently he wrote a bad report on my record card at the end of my month's training, notwithstanding the rollicking he delivered in front of everyone in the cage every time I returned after bunking off.

My two weeks with the testing man were much better spent and I learnt a lot about peak volts, cranking torques and the correct performance of magnetos and other ancillary electrical equipment.

This chap was much younger than the others who worked in the sparky's cage and he was quite keen on practical jokes too.

The most common magneto we dealt with was the Scintilla Vertex, which was fitted to the Scarabs and Mechanical Horses. They were fantastic units, capable of producing a hefty fat spark with only a quarter of a turn of the armature. On occasions, the testing man would attach one of the magneto's high tension leads to the metal bench and run the unit up on the test rig. Anyone then touching the bench would be subjected to a 20,000 volt shock. There was virtually no amperage of course, but nevertheless it gave a pretty hefty jolt, which could be quite painful. Naturally the testing man and his apprentice would make sure they were well clear of the bench, thus avoiding any consequences.

If Bill received a shock he would know immediately who was responsible and, without turning round, shout out in his broad accent, "We're here to work, not play bloody daft games, now cut it out or I'll have you upstairs."

'Upstairs' meant in front of the chief road motor engineer for a dressing down.

A month with Frank, the general electrician, was well worth having to put up with Bill's curmudgeonly ways and I would have liked to have spent more time repairing electrical faults on actual vehicles, but it was not to be. The plan for training apprentices had been set before the war, when vehicle electrics were very crude, and a month, they had determined, was time enough for anyone. At the time of my apprenticeship, vehicle electrics were advancing by leaps and bounds and were much more complex than ever before. However, 'rules is rules' and one month was all any apprentice was going to get repairing vehicle electrics on the actual vehicles.

Electrician Frank was a Lancastrian, very soft spoken and sometimes quite aloof, but he was a brilliant auto electrician who could find any fault, rewire a vehicle and manufacture a simple wiring loom in no time at all.

When it came to looms, we would strip out the old, often burnt out, wiring loom from the vehicle, take it to the sparky's cage where we would remove all the binding tape and measure the length, note the colour and add a label indicating the function of each wire. Then, consulting the appropriate wiring diagram in the workshop manual, we would proceed to cut lengths of the appropriately coloured electrical wire from the numerous reels of the stuff we kept in the cage. Then, using a large flat plywood board attached to the side of the cage and some panel pins, we would construct a former or template upon which the wires could be laid out in the same way as the original loom. Then, using fresh binding tape we would complete the job, and, hey presto, a new loom in about a day.

This was all excellent training and I was sorry to leave Frank because there was so much to learn and I know I could have absorbed a lot more of it too.

My two weeks with the chap who looked after the battery cage, commonly known as 'The Gas Chamber' (it was a different time then and political correctness had not been invented) by all the apprentices, was both instructive and life-threatening. It was situated next door to the sparky's cage and shielded from it and the cage beyond by steel panels. This was to prevent the stink and fumes of the sulphuric acid and molten pitch, used in the refurbishment of batteries, from gassing everyone in the vicinity. On the end wall, which faced Duddeston Mill Road, there was a fan two feet in diameter set into a hole which ran day and night to dispel the acid and pitch fumes from the hell that was the battery cage.

Near the door there was a large battery charger which was capable of charging about a dozen batteries all at once. When a number of batteries were being charged at the same time, the fumes given off would catch in the back of your throat, regardless of what the fan was doing. The fumes were also highly flammable, so smoking and naked flames were prohibited.

Further into the cage was the area where new plates were fitted to the batteries. This entailed emptying the electrolyte from the battery into an old ceramic sink, there being an empty acid carboy under the plughole to catch the dangerous mixture of sulphuric acid and distilled water. Then carefully melting and scraping away the pitch that sealed the top of the batteries using a large electric soldering iron and a scraper. Once free, the old plates were lifted out and disposed of in a drum of water. The inside of the ebonite (also known as vulcanite) battery case was then thoroughly cleaned out and the new plates fitted before resealing the top of the battery with fresh pitch, which was always simmering happily in a cauldron on an electric hot plate near the front of the cage. New electrolyte would be mixed, bearing in mind that you must always add sulphuric acid very slowly to water, not water to acid, or there could be an almighty explosion. We apprentices learnt this little snippet of information very quickly, some by bitter experience. Finally, the re-plated battery would be refilled and charged.

When carrying out a battery plate change it was necessary to wear a thick leather apron, thick leather elbow-length gloves and what can only be described as a World War II gas mask. The whole getup was very uncomfortable and very restrictive. No wonder some apprentices spilt electrolyte all over the place, it was very difficult to see through the steamed up goggles of the gas mask.

I did a couple of plate change jobs quite successfully in my two weeks there, but that was enough for me. The discomfort and danger from the pitch fumes and electrolyte was overwhelming, despite the fan in the wall. The design of battery that could be repaired in this way was disappearing fast, even then, and I was quite happy with this march of technology. By the time I had finished my apprenticeship in 1963, re-plating vehicle batteries had been consigned to the history books.

You could always tell which apprentice was in the battery cage by simply looking at his overalls. They would be full of holes where splashes of electrolyte had burnt through the material. Amazingly, it only took a minute or two to ruin a perfectly good pair of overalls. His trousers and shirt underneath would be holed as well, much to his mother's consternation when he got home. I know this from first hand experience.

All in all the sparky's cage was enlightening and instructive, despite the somewhat unorthodox training from certain quarters and the risk of being dissolved by acid. However, it quickly dawned on me that I really didn't want to have too much to do with vehicle electrics. The mechanical bits were far more interesting as far as I was concerned.

At the end of the year Mr Goodman was in the habit of inviting the apprentices into his office one by one to go over their report cards from the various sections they had worked in during that period. When it was my turn to face the music, I sat quietly and apprehensively whilst Mr Goodman read through my card.

"You're doing very well, Ken, but you seem to have slipped up in the sparky's cage with Bill. Anything you want to say about that?"

I had a feeling that Bill had given me a bad report, so I decided to come clean and replied that it could be boring just standing around watching someone else do all the work and that's why I would disappear for an hour or so every now and then. Quickly adding that I was not just scrounging when I absented myself, I was watching and talking to others about their work.

"OK, lad, don't worry about it. Bill gives all the apprentices a bad report because he's a cantankerous old bugger who thinks he's the only one who knows how to do anything electrical, but I never said that. All right?"

Quite relieved, I smiled and nodded.

Chapter 8
BOOK LEARNING

Around the beginning of September every year, Mr Goodman issued a memo warning the apprentices that it would soon be time to sign up for night school or day release. When everyone was sufficiently aware and had ensured that they had the money to pay the registration fee, we would be rounded up and told to board a 40 seat crew bus that Mr Goodman always borrowed from the Permanent Way Department next door. Ernie Ellerman would then drive us round the city picking up the apprentices from the district workshops. When the full complement was all present and correct, Ernie would drive us to Aston Technical College in Whitehead Road. The college would have been consulted beforehand and a day fixed for the registration of railway apprentices, since there could be up to 20 of us arriving to register all at the same time.

The younger apprentices, like me, signed up for the City and Guilds Mechanics Certificate course. A three year period of instruction covering Workshop Practice, Motor Vehicle Technology and Motor Vehicle Calculations and Science. It required three nights per week from 7pm to 9pm during the period September to May. The more senior apprentices, having already attained their Mechanics Certificate, would sign up for the City and Guilds Technicians Certificate course, which required a further two years of study. However, they were lucky because they were permitted to attend college for one day per week to complete the course, which made life much easier for them.

When college started, I settled into a routine and quite enjoyed attending. Some of my fellow apprentices were not comfortable being back in a classroom situation and it sometimes showed in their results. I had no such qualms and quickly knuckled down to learn all I could about the theory of motor vehicle engineering.

It was a bit of a pain to get to Aston Tech, as it was colloquially known, and sometimes I really didn't feel much like sitting there for two hours after a really trying or tough day at work. My usual plan was to leave directly from the workshop at 5pm and catch the number eight inner circle bus at Saltley Gate. On reaching Park Lane I would alight from the bus and walk down Selston Road to Whitehead Road, a distance of about a quarter of a mile. Thankfully, the college had an excellent refectory, so my cooked evening meal would be purchased there at a very reasonable price.

Getting back home after 9pm entailed catching the number eight bus again, but in the opposite direction back to Saltley Gate, where I would transfer to a number 14 bus to The Bull's Head pub in Stechford and walk up the hill past Parkinson's factory to Frederick Road. By the time I reached home exhaustion had frequently overtaken me and I would often just go to bed almost immediately.

I got through the three years of night school and achieved a first class pass in the Mechanics exam. This entitled me to attend further college courses on a day release basis and this is what happened for the Technicians course, which made life so much easier and less exhausting. Having achieved a first class pass in the Technicians exam too, I was then entitled to move on and sign up for the Ordinary National Certificate (ONC) in mechanical engineering, which then led to the Higher National Certificate (HNC). Both of which I achieved with distinction.

Later, when I had finished my time and left the railways, I was given the opportunity to become a part-time lecturer in Workshop Practice and Motor Vehicle Technology at Handsworth Technical College, just off the Soho Road. This was something I enjoyed immensely, not to mention the extra £2-18s-6d (approximately £2.92) it added to my income.

Despite being poorly educated at Bierton Road, I managed to secure a formal education in motor vehicle and general mechanical engineering. Though it was achieved the hard way, through night school, day release and it occupied ten years of my early life, I would do it all over again. To me it was more valuable than gold and it served me well for the whole of my working life. However, the most satisfying thing of all was the fact that it was all paid for by British Railways, who reimbursed all my registration fees, course fees and exam fees even after I had completed my apprenticeship. An excellent result, I would say.

Chapter 9
I BECOME MOBILE

As soon as I was 16, I acquired a provisional licence and a motorcycle. It was a 1939 Frances Barnet 125cc two stroke, with a hand-change gearbox, rigid frame and girder forks. It cost me five pounds (almost a month's wages) and a few more shillings to bring it up to scratch.

My mother was not very happy about my acquisition, but, after some heated discussion, she agreed that I could ride it on the condition that I wore a crash helmet. This was long before the law demanded crash helmets, but I was happy to wear the one that my mother bought for me as a belated birthday present because it seemed like a sensible thing to do.

Though petrol had gone up in price in December 1956 by an unbelievable one shilling and fivepence (7p) per gallon, due to the Suez Crisis, it was still worth occasionally using the bike for work. On the three evenings that I had to attend night school, I would motorcycle to work in the morning thus affording myself much more flexibility in getting to the college in the evening. More importantly, getting home at night no longer relied on waiting for buses when classes had finished at 9pm.

I passed my motorcycle driving test a few months after buying the Frances Barnet and as my wages increased, so I aspired to bigger and better motorcycles (with some help from my parents in the early days). My next purchase was a 1955 model Triumph 199cc Tiger Cub, an excellent machine. Then I bought a 1960 model single cylinder 500cc AJS (with the 'jam-pot' rear suspension), which I rode for many years. My final bike was a magnificent 1950 model 1000cc Ariel Square Four, with a double adult sidecar to accommodate my growing family. Later, having already obtained my car driving licence at the age of 17, I moved on to four wheels. However, I will always look upon my time as a motorcyclist as happy, happy days, despite coming off several times in the wet when riding along the cobbled streets that were so common in the city at that time.

Chapter 10
THE TYRE CAGE (DANNY'S CAGE)
January 1958 to April 1958

When Mr Goodman told me I had finished in the battery cage and was to report to the tyre cage, I was both relieved and puzzled. *How long does it take to learn about big black round things with a hole in the middle?* I wondered. *Not three months, surely?* I was to be surprised.

When I reported for duty on the Monday morning, Danny, who was in charge of the tyre cage, was squatting on top of the workbench eating an apple. He acknowledged me and said he would be with me in a moment. I stood looking at him with some amazement. As he clambered off the bench to throw the apple core into the waste bin, I could see that he was of average height with long arms and a barrel chest. The surprising thing about him was the amount of hair on his head, arms and chest, all of which were exposed because his sleeves were rolled up, the front of his overalls were open to just below his waist and he wore no shirt underneath. His hair was black, but turning to grey and it reminded me of the famous photograph of Albert Einstein, it was so frizzed up. His chest was a carpet of black/grey hairs making it impossible to see any sign of skin. Danny looked like the wild man of Borneo without the facial hair and he moved around with amazing simian-like agility. I reckoned he was in his early 40s, but he could have been older.

It was January and quite cold; the workshop where the cages were situated was heated by hot water pipes feeding large radiators fixed to the roof girders. The radiators had fans to blow hot air down upon us. Despite these numerous heating units, the workshop could still be quite cool because of the vehicle access doors opening and closing all day long. Consequently, most people wore a jumper or similar garment under their overalls to keep warm in the winter. Not Danny, he stripped down to his underpants every morning and just wore his overalls, but open all the way down his front. He was forever complaining about the heat, even in the depths of winter. When he changed to go home, he only ever wore a shirt, trousers and a light linen jacket, no matter how cold it was.

I found out that Danny was a Welshman from Swansea and that he was incredibly strong, able to move huge wheels and tyres around with no effort. His easy going manner and willingness to teach all he knew about inner tubes, tyres and tyre valves made him an extremely likable bloke, despite his quirky ways. He was a vegetarian and he told me once that he had never knowingly eaten meat. In fact, he always used to make some comment or other when we settled down at the back of the cage to eat our lunch. He would first watch me take out a ham or corned beef sandwich and then say in his sing-song Welsh accent, "That bloody stuff will kill you if you keep eating it, boyo. Poisoning your body you are, see."

I would always reply, "Yes, Danny, but it's ever so nice," and laugh.

The other thing about Danny was that I never saw him drink anything other than plain tap water. What dedication.

I soon realised that there was more to tyres and tubes than meets the eye, as Danny set about showing me how to deal with them safely and correctly. From huge mobile crane wheels with locking rings to retain the massive balloon tyres, right down to private car tyres that simply slipped over the rim with a bit of force and some soft soap, Danny held forth on each and made it all seem so easy. In those days there were virtually no tubeless tyres, so I was taught how to detect and repair punctures that would last the lifetime of the inner tube. We had all the appropriate machinery in the cage, most of which was operated pneumatically and you really needed to watch your fingers when removing tyres from rims using these machines. Right at the back of the cage was a huge water tank for leak testing and, on more than one occasion, especially in the hot summers, Danny was sometimes observed using it as a plunge pool to keep cool.

The other piece of important equipment was a special reinforced cage in which the really large commercial vehicle tyres could be inflated with absolute safety. Many commercial vehicle manufactures employed the locking ring method of keeping tyres on the rims. It's like a giant circlip and has to be seated properly otherwise it can blow off the rim when inflating the tyre, with devastating consequences. It was mandatory therefore that when inflating tyres fitted for the first time on a locking ring rim, the whole assembly had to be placed in this special cage so that if the locking ring came off it would not injure or kill the person inflating the tyre.

The other thing I had really not expected were the days out in a small van, when Danny and I would be summoned to one of the many railway goods yards dotted around the city to change a wheel on a truck or crane because of a puncture. Danny was a bit of an erratic driver, but nonetheless the days out were a real tonic and I learnt how to jack and secure all makes and models, from huge Walker Brothers 10 ton mobile cranes to little Ford vans, safely and quickly to enable wheels to be changed.

Towards the end of my three months with Danny, the management had purchased a tyre tread re-cutting machine and naturally they asked Danny to test it. The machine was a hand held, electrically heated cutter with a special U-shaped blade that could cut new grooves in worn tyres to supposedly make them legal again. We both made numerous attempts to make it work properly, but to no avail. The resulting tread pattern would be erratic and vary in depth, simply because the machine was hand controlled. Danny made his report and the machine was soon taken away by one of the district managers from upstairs and we never heard anything about it again. Even if it had been successful, I couldn't imagine that anyone would be happy to drive a heavy truck on re-cut tyre treads. In fact, Danny and I concluded that even then it was probably illegal to cut new treads in old tyres, it certainly is now.

I had never met a man like Danny before and when I left the tyre cage to go to the welding cage next door, I knew I would miss that quirky, hairy free spirited Welshman.

Chapter 11
THE WELDING CAGE (GEORGE'S PLACE)
April 1958 to July 1958

The man in control of the welding cage was a completely different kettle of fish to Danny. He was brusque, dominating and loud, though in a friendly and jokey sort of way. Whilst everyone else on the shop floor wore blue boiler suits, George insisted on wearing a brown boiler suit. He was about 60 years old and totally bald, which he was very sensitive about. Consequently, he wore a French beret all the time when at work, quickly changing it for a flat cap when it was time to go home. We apprentices liked to spy on him at clocking off time, just to watch him do the lightening-quick slight of hand act with his flat cap. However, if he caught you watching him it was necessary to depart quickly because you could more or less guarantee that a hammer or a pair of heavy-duty tongs would soon be flying out of his cage. Though he would call his apprentices all sorts of names when they made mistakes, it was done in a friendly manner; there really was no serious aggression with George, it was all a front.

He was just over five feet tall, quite plump and always wore a sardonic smile on his face; in fact he would have made a very good substitute for Arthur Lowe (Captain Mainwaring of *Dad's Army* fame. A British TV comedy series about the Home Guard during the war, which began in the late 1960s and was recently made into a full length film in 2015), such was his resemblance to that actor.

All the gas welding, electric arc welding and heavy-duty brazing undertaken in our workshops came under George's jurisdiction. Sometimes he was even called upon to carry out welding operations on the locomotives in the loco sheds next door.

He was generous with his knowledge and showed me how to gas weld with oxy-acetylene sets and the importance of gas pressures and nozzle size selection for the different thicknesses of metal to be joined. I was also introduced to electric arc welding, which was necessary for the really heavy-duty chassis repairs we sometimes undertook. However, the routine day-to-day work of the welding cage was the repair of aluminium castings, such as engine sumps and gearbox casings; the welding of cracked cast iron cylinder blocks and axle housings and the brazing of exhaust manifolds, where the retaining lugs had broken off. Like the other cages, George operated an exchange system for the more common welding repairs.

I found welding aluminium using oxy-acetylene the most difficult of all. You could hold the torch over the crack to be welded and nothing would seem to happen until suddenly that part of the casting simply collapsed in a heap on the bench. It was then that George would call me all sorts of things and gently shove me out of the way to examine the damage.

His favourite admonishment was, "You'll never make a bloody welder as long as you've got a hole in your arse, you dozy, dozy boy."

He would then try to recover the damage and tell me to have another go. After about a week of constantly trying to weld aluminium, I did get the hang of it. The secret, George had revealed, was to watch the colour of the material just adjacent to where the heat was being applied. When it began to turn a barely perceptible pale blue colour; that was when the welding rod could be applied to fill the V-shaped groove that had been cut along the length of the crack to achieve weld penetration and thus unite the material.

George spent a lot of time showing me how to achieve a really neat weld, be it gas, arc or brazing. According to him it showed proficiency, professionalism and it produced a sound weld; and he was right. There was nothing more likely to turn someone off a repair than a weld that looked as if it had been smeared on like cold, lumpy porridge.

Moving the big heavy gas bottles was quite a challenge in the early days of my time with George. He, on the other hand, could grab the neck of an empty oxygen bottle as tall as himself and twirl it round with his other hand as if he were dancing with it. In no time at all he would have it at the side of the British Oxygen Company's truck, ready for the driver to load it. It was exactly the same with the much shorter and stubby acetylene bottles too. After a few tries I managed to shift the bottles reasonably quickly, but I would never be in George's league; that was a given.

If one of the apprentices from the service workshop or overhaul shop came to the welding cage with a request and didn't ask nicely (no apprentice ever did 'ask nicely' as far as George was concerned), he would grab a hammer and beat it down several times on the steel-topped bench making an enormously loud noise and invite the boy to 'go away' immediately. This action always brought on a whole series of cat-calls and laughter from the men in the workshop as George stood at the entrance to his cage shouting after the unfortunate apprentice, "Piss off you cheeky little bugger and don't come back until you've learnt some bloody manners."

The lad, and everyone else, knew that George was only joking and the boy would return later, apologise (with tongue firmly in cheek) and get his request fulfilled. Sometimes, however, we apprentices would contrive such incidents just to hear George in full flow. What tormentors we were.

Despite all his bluster and bawling, George was a kindly man at heart. In fact, when I had finished my apprenticeship a few years later, he told me that he only ever took the mickey, cursed and shouted at the lads he actually liked.

I learnt a lot about welding, brazing, banter and swearing from George and it paid off later when I came top in the 1963 National Craftsman's practical examination for the West Midlands. It was my welding and brazing that clinched it for me. Thanks George, you were a real diamond.

Chapter 12
THE MACHINE SHOP
July 1958 to January 1959

The machine shop was the last of what I called the peripheral stages of my training to be a motor fitter, and I transferred to this department in mid-July 1958. The man in charge was named Reginald, known to all and sundry as plain old 'Reggie'. He was of average height, but very thin and I suspect he was well into his 60s. It was noticeable that he had reached a stage in his life where he had to slow down a little. Notwithstanding his physical frailties, his mind was as sharp as a knife and he could complete quite complex mathematical problems in his head whilst I was still writing them down and reaching for my slide rule. His knowledge and dexterity in operating machine tools was legendary and he was ever willing to pass on his knowledge to the apprentices.

Reggie was the only man in the machine shop, apart from his apprentice of course, but he kept up a good pace in resurfacing engine flywheels and clutch faceplates for the overhaul shop, skimming up the commutators on starter and dynamo armatures for the sparky's cage and carrying out all the cylinder block re-bores when required. Again, just like all the cages, the machine shop ran an exchange scheme for the more common refurbishments and serviced all the requirements of the district workshops too, so there was plenty to do.

In addition to this routine activity, Reggie was sometimes required to manufacture certain parts that were no longer available from the manufacturers. For example, the little petrol-driven tractor units that ran around the platforms at New Street station towing four-wheeled parcel trolleys were manufactured in the late 1920s and utilised the same engine as the famous bull-nosed Morris car. Parts were no longer available for these machines, therefore it was up to Reggie and his apprentice to manufacture, within reason, whatever was required.

Through my own interest in the work and Reggie's patient tutoring, I soon mastered lathe work and the shaping machine, plus all the maths associated with such work. Therefore, he could leave me to my own devices knowing I wouldn't make a mess of whatever job I was doing. Later, I was able to take on the re-bores and cylinder honing jobs, working to great accuracy to ensure the oversized pistons would fit correctly into the refurbished cylinders. However, when it came to working with the radial drilling machine, I would often come unstuck.

For several weeks Reggie would not permit me to use the machine on actual jobs. He would only allow me to practice on scraps of metal, drilling various sized holes at precise distances from each other. Then he would check my work and point out to me that I was several thousandths of an inch out of true regarding the relative positions of the holes. This happened time and time again and I began to wonder if the drill was true.

I was well aware of the old maxim, 'A bad workman always blames his tools', so I kept quiet about my suspicions for a while. After a constant flow of failed drilling operations, I noticed that Reggie always had a smile on his face when he was pointing out my mistakes. My suspicions began to grow.

Finally I said, "There's something wrong with that radial driller, isn't there Reggie?"

He smiled and then came clean, "You're right, our kid. The pillar bearings are worn, so the drilling head sags slightly. It's only a few thou, but it's enough to put any hole you drill a fraction out from where it should be."

He then proceeded to show me his technique for getting it right. By moving the work to be drilled a few thou forward of the drill head in line with the axis of the drill arm, it was possible, with practice, to compensate for the inaccuracy of the machine. When I asked him why the machine couldn't be repaired or replaced, he simply told me to look at the date on the manufacture's plate attached to the pillar. I don't remember the maker's name, but the date of manufacture was 1895, enough said. Everyone knew the railways were in a very poor financial state at that time, so the chance of getting a new radial driller was pretty much zero.

We had a good laugh over it and Reggie told me that I was one of only three previous apprentices who had had the courage to question the accuracy of the machine. He surprised me a little when he said, in true Sherlock Holmes style, "If you've checked all your calculations and your settings and the job still comes out wrong, then you need to start thinking about the integrity of your machine."

Clearly Reggie had been testing me to see if I could work out what was wrong, and it pleased me somewhat to know that I had found the problem, eventually.

There was a spark plug cleaning and testing machine in the machine shop and it was generally acknowledged as the apprentice's job to clean the spark plugs and check the gaps when servicing a vehicle. Consequently, I would often see lads doing this work and was able to observe quietly the tricks some of the fitters used to play on these poor apprentices.

While no one was using the machine, one of the fitters would come along with a piece of wire and connect the body of the machine to the high voltage terminal that was used to test for sparks at the plug electrodes. Then if anyone came along, didn't notice the wire and pressed the test button, the whole machine became live and the poor devil operating it received about 20,000 volts through his body (as per the magneto trick in the sparky's cage). Having observed this jolly prank on several occasions, I was wary from then on and always searched for the wire when it was my turn to use the machine after transferring to the vehicle repair workshop a few months later.

Chapter 13
AN UNFORTUNATE OCCURRENCE

Just before I left the machine shop in January 1959, a group of us apprentices were eating our lunch time sandwiches around one of the two huge pot-bellied coal burning stoves that helped to heat the chippie's shop, the overhaul workshop and the machine shop.

Because of the overhead crane in the overhaul shop, it was not possible to employ the overhead radiator and fan system that heated the repair workshop. To supplement the heat that simply wafted in from the repair workshop, these powerful stoves were absolutely essential in winter. I suspect they were actually there first, when the building was erected around 1900, long before the radiator and fan system was installed. The stoves were lit every winter morning by one of the labourers who came in early primarily to light the furnace that powered the overhead radiator system. I watched him carry out these duties one morning after coming in early because I was to act as a driver's mate for Mr Ellerman in returning a Walker Brothers 10 ton mobile crane back to its goods yard in the Black Country (more of this later).

The labourer acquired a four-wheeled trolley and placed some steel sheeting on the wooden platform and wheeled it over to the fire pit in the loco sheds. This was where the loco cleaners dumped the contents of the fireboxes from the locomotives before preparing them for overhaul or repair. He scooped up a couple of shovels full of almost white-hot coal embers and deposited them on the steel sheeting he had placed on the trolley. He then wheeled it to the furnace that powered the radiator system and quickly shovelled the glowing embers into it, added more coal and nursed the fire into life by manipulating the dampers. Satisfied that the furnace was alight, he collected hot embers for each of the stoves in the overhaul shop and lit those fires in a similar fashion. Within about 20 minutes he had everything powered up and burning brightly. I'm sure it would have taken a couple of hours if he'd had to light the fires from scratch. Thank goodness for the fire pit, so conveniently located in the loco sheds.

It was really cold on this particular day as we huddled around the stove eagerly consuming our lunches. The heat from it was so intense that the cast iron body was glowing dull red in places and it made our overalls steam at a distance of about five or six feet. Unusually, Reggie had joined us, he was telling a story about the early days of the RMED and I, having finished my sandwiches, was rooting around for the apple my mother usually placed in my bag. There was no apple, but I did find an orange and I remember thinking how unusual that was since they were still quite hard to get. I took it out and began to peel it when Reggie suddenly stopped talking and turned to look at me.

"Is that a bloody orange?" he cried looking very worried.

"Yes, it's just my lunch," I replied, wondering what the problem was.

One of the older apprentices pointed at me and said, "You've done it now, dimwit."

With that, Reggie almost ran from our group retching and heaving. He managed to get to the Duddeston Mill Road set of doors and it was there that I found him being sick in the little yard beyond. I still had the orange in my hand and Reggie immediately shouted, "Get rid of that bloody orange."

I threw the half-eaten orange over the adjacent wall into the canal that ran at the back of our workshop and asked Reggie what was wrong.

"Go and wash your hands and I will speak to you later. I'm all right now," he replied.

I left him standing there breathing fresh air and headed to the washroom, wondering how an orange could cause such a reaction. It wasn't that he'd eaten any of it; it seemed to be just the pungent smell that had set him off.

I returned to the machine shop after thoroughly washing my hands and rubbing Rozalex (an industrial hand protector and cleaner) all over them in an attempt to smother the smell of oranges.

Reggie was standing next to the radial driller smoking a cigarette as I approached him.

"Have you got rid of that awful stink, lad?"

I told him that I had washed my hands and applied Rozalex to mask the smell and he seemed satisfied.

I said that I was really sorry and had I known that the smell of oranges would elicit such a reaction from him, I would never have started to peel it in his company. He began by telling me that he should have mentioned it, but since he had not seen me eat an orange before this incident, he had thought no more about it. Reggie seemed to have recovered somewhat and the colour had returned to his face, so I thought it appropriate to ask him why he had reacted to the smell in such a violent way. The story he told me was quite amazing.

Reggie had been an artilleryman in the First World War and in the late summer of 1917, his battery, along with other British forces, found themselves on the Italian Front at the Piave River supporting the Italian army against the Austrians. Reggie and his colleagues had been ordered to set up their battery in an orange grove, but very early the next morning the Austrian artillery began an intensive, long range barrage on their positions. The battery was virtually obliterated by high explosives and Reggie was one of only half a dozen survivors. When the Austrian guns stopped, all Reggie and his few remaining mates could see were the smashed guns, the mangled bodies of their comrades and the matchwood that had once been a pleasant orange grove. The smell of cordite, blood and oranges that remained for hours after the bombardment was so powerful that Reggie had never been able to forget it. Since that dramatic, life-changing day in 1917, the smell of oranges would rekindle the memory of the incident and make him physically sick.

As he finished telling me about it, I could see that he was on the verge of tears and had a very strained expression on his face, so I made an excuse and left him to his memories.

Thinking about it later, I could only wonder at the horror he must have witnessed on that awful day.

Strangely enough, I never took an orange to work after that and I rarely eat one even now, nearly 60 years after first hearing the story from Reggie.

I left the machine shop in mid-January 1959, with a good working knowledge of precision lathe work, shaping, boring and grinding. As I had come to expect of my various masters, Reggie imparted his knowledge freely and with pride, and for that I shall be ever grateful because it helped to build my confidence and make me a better craftsman.

Chapter 14
MY DAY AS A DRIVER'S MATE

Around Christmas time in 1958, Mr Goodman asked me if I would like to accompany Ernie Ellerman when he returned a Walker Brothers mobile crane to Wolverhampton the following morning. Eager to do anything new, I agreed immediately. Though, as it turned out, I didn't quite understand the duties expected of a driver's mate in the case of this crane. Smiling, Mr Goodman told me to go and find Ernie and tell him that I was nominated for the job.

I had visions of a comfortable ride in a warm cab, indulging in casual discussions with Ernie and having a pleasant day out of the workshop for a change. How wrong could anyone be?

"Make sure you wrap up warm Ken, there's no heater in that crane. All you get is the warm air from the engine wafting back into the cab."

I nodded and said that I would make sure I had enough warm clothing for the trip. This was the first disappointing aspect of the job.

We both agreed to get the early train from Stechford, thus enabling us to arrive at the workshop by about 7am, giving us time to check over the crane and depart just before 8am. Ernie was a stickler for proper procedures and checking to see that the vehicle was fully roadworthy was only to be expected, despite the fact that it had just been overhauled.

The following morning we met on the platform and travelled on the early train to Adderley Park. As we were walking down the road towards the RMED workshops, Ernie began to acquaint me with my duties for the day.

He explained that the crane we were returning to its goods yard had a ratchet-wheel type handbrake that took several pulls of the lever to wind a cable round a drum to apply the brakes securely. Therefore, when we stopped at traffic lights, junctions or simply because of congestion and there was an appreciable gradient, it was my job to jump out of the cab and apply a heavy-duty wooden chock to one of the wheels. The idea being to stop the vehicle from rolling backwards or forwards, depending on which way the gradient sloped. The application of the chock would give Ernie time to ratchet the handbrake on without having to worry about trying to keep his foot on the normal brake pedal or rolling into any other vehicles in the vicinity. If the road was level, Ernie indicated, he would be able to cope well enough without the chock.

"So, all you have to do is anticipate the gradient, jump out, quickly apply the chock until I tell you to remove it and all will be well. Is that clear?" said Ernie, awaiting a positive response from me.

This was the second disappointment regarding this job and I asked why he couldn't just hold the crane on the footbrake and forget all about the chocking business.

"The chock is simply a safety precaution and, as you know, I'm all for safety as far as driving is concerned. You see, the crane has a huge counterweight that makes it so heavy, the effort required on the footbrake is immense and it might take me a few seconds to get the handbrake on tight enough, so I want the chock applied on gradients, just in case. It's a crane, and it's usually confined to a level goods yard where hill starts are rarely encountered. It spends most of the day with its stabilisers out, off-loading railway wagons; the brakes are hardly ever used."

True enough; the mobile crane was based on a normal six-wheeled commercial vehicle chassis running on balloon tyres with a heavily reinforced frame and a huge counterweight to enable it to lift 10 tons. Little wonder the footbrake needed so much pressure and the hand brake required a ratchet-wheel to apply enough force to hold it. Releasing the handbrake was easy and immediate; it came off as soon as the trigger on the lever was pulled, like any conventional handbrake.

I indicated to Ernie that I now understood what the problem was and my role in solving it. He simply replied that I would soon get used to it.

After checking the crane over in our workshop, Ernie and I set off for Wolverhampton goods yard, but as we began to move gently down the slope from the RMED workshops into Duddeston Mill Road, it began to rain. This was my third disappointment with this job.

I jumped out of the cab at the bottom of the slope and applied the heavy chock to the front of one of the front wheels, while Ernie pumped the handbrake lever vigorously to hold the crane on the slope. Then, at Ernie's signal, I tried to pull the chock away by its long wooden handle, but it was held fast by the tyre. I shouted that it was stuck and Ernie shouted back that I would have to waggle it about. After a few hefty waggles it came out and I clambered back into the cab.

"Is that how it's going to be all the way to Wolverhampton?" I queried.

"Yes. As I said, you'll get used to it," replied Ernie, smiling.

The maximum speed of the vehicle was no more than 25 miles per hour and our route to Wolverhampton took us through the heart of the Birmingham and Black Country conurbations, with dozens of traffic lights, junctions and hills. Though our destination was only about 20 miles away from Saltley, it took us the best part of four hours to complete the journey.

I can't remember how many times I had to jump out of the relatively warm cab to apply the chock, but I do recall that on my arrival at the goods yard in Wolverhampton, my arms were aching like mad because of all the waggling it required to release it and I was soaked. The rain had not let up for one moment throughout the trip. Furthermore, I had been verbally abused by so many drivers because they were stuck behind us as we crawled through the congested streets, that I almost forgot my real name. They would see me jump down from the cab to apply the chock and realise that I was more or less a captive audience for their displeasure; hence they took full advantage of that fact.

By the time we had handed the crane over to the goods yard foreman and received a signature for it, I was thoroughly exhausted, not to mention soaked by rain and miserably cold. Ernie said we should go to the goods yard mess room to dry out. When we arrived, I was heartened to see that there was a roaring fire blazing away in a cast iron stove and the mess room was as warm as toast. Once I was dry, thoroughly warmed up and we had eaten our sandwiches, Ernie and I made our way to the railway station and caught the train back to Saltley, utilising the special passes that Mr Goodman had prepared for us.

The following day my arms still ached from all the heaving that was required to release the chock and I reminded myself never to volunteer for anything ever again. By way of compensation, there was an extra sixpence (2.5p) in my wage packet the following week. It was my overtime for the extra hour I had put in getting to the workshop early.

THE NEXT THIRTY-SIX MONTHS
(January 1959 to January 1962)

Here are a few of the headlines that worried or pleased us from this period of time.

August 1959
Alec Issigonis launches the Austin/Morris Mini.

October 1959
Harold Macmillan leads Tories to victory in General Election.

June 1960
Jaguar takes over the Daimler car company.

December 1960
National Service comes to an end with the last intake.

January 1961
The one-millionth Morris Minor is produced.

April 1961
Britain applies to join the Common Market.

Mr Goodman thought it was time for me to "Get down to the meat of things," as he termed it. My next assignment would be 18 months in the overhaul workshop, overhauling engines, front suspensions, gearboxes and rear axles from all makes and models of trucks, buses and cars. Later, I would move on to the complete vehicle overhaul shop for nine months where all the engine and transmission units were stripped out, the body removed and the chassis de-scaled and refurbished, ready for the re-fitment of the overhauled units. The work covered a wide range of vehicles and there was plenty to be done too, since we were the central workshops and received vehicles and units for overhaul from all the district workshops in the city. What a challenge it was.

Chapter 15
THE ENGINE OVERHAUL WORKSHOP
January 1959 to January 1960

My first master was named Jack and he lived in Brownhills. He owned a wonderfully maintained 1950 Jowett Javelin car which reflected his pedantic nature in the way it sparkled brightly, even in the depths of winter. Jack had the reputation for being a highly skilled and very meticulous engine fitter. We would receive engines of all shapes and sizes from all over the city and these would be stripped of their ancillary items, such as the starter motors and dynamos, which were then delivered to the sparky's cage for attention. Then the engine was completely dismantled, the resulting bits and pieces were dispatched to the labourers who would load the parts into wire baskets and immerse everything in a huge Trichloroethylene tank (known as the gunk tank) to clean off the oil and dirt. When the parts were returned to us we would inspect them carefully and order new parts where necessary. On receipt of the new parts from the stores we would proceed to rebuild the engine.

Often the cylinder block would require re-boring, so it would be sent to Reggie for him, or his apprentice, to deal with. On some of the very old Scammell Mechanical Horse engines, which dated back to the 1930s, the crankshaft and connecting rod bearings were of the cast white metal kind and had to be melted out with a blowtorch, recast with new white metal in special formers and then accurately line-bored to within a thousandth of an inch.

The large diesel engines fitted to some of the really heavy trucks and buses had to be handled by the overhead crane every time they were moved, such was their size and weight. Some engines were tiny 100cc two stoke motors attached to the rail drillers that were used by the permanent way gangs to drill holes in railway lines on site. Other engines were so old that the parts had to be manufactured by Reggie or salvaged from scrap engines. They included some of the single cylinder Lister diesels dating back to 1931, which were also used by the permanent way gangs to obtain rotary power at the trackside or to drive water pumps and generators.

As I have mentioned, Jack was a meticulous fitter, so he expected his apprentice to be meticulous too. This was no problem for me because I wanted to learn how to overhaul engines correctly and apply sound engineering principles when doing so. However, one of Jack's little fetishes, of which he had many, was particularly irritating, time consuming and made no difference whatsoever to the quality or integrity of the rebuilt engine.

I don't want to bore the reader, so I shall keep the following description as brief as possible, but hopefully still comprehensible.

The main bearing caps that hold the crankshaft into the engine block/crankcase are usually held down by utilising large studs threaded into the crankcase. In those days all of these studs would have a small hole drilled through near the top of the thread to accommodate a split pin, which stopped the castellated retaining nut from working loose due to the vibrations of the engine.

Now, when these studs were screwed into the crankcase during initial assembly at the factory, the position of the split pin holes could occupy any direction through 360 degrees. This was not good enough for Jack; he would insist that the split pin holes must all face in exactly the same direction, i.e. in line with the crankshaft. If they weren't in line with the crankshaft, and let's face it they generally were not, then it was the apprentice's job to see that they were.

The studs had to be extracted and have a little more thread carefully cut by either filing or using a thread cutting die so that the stud could be screwed into the crankcase a little further to enable the split pin holes to point in exactly the same direction. Of course, if the stud 'bottomed' in the hole, then the base of the stud had to be filed too.

Bearing in mind that a four cylinder engine could have six or ten such studs, depending on its design, and if they all needed attention the work could take a couple of hours. Quite naturally the apprentice would, on some occasions, make a complete mess of re-cutting the thread of one or two studs, which then necessitated drawing new ones from the stores or asking Reggie to manufacture replacements from round steel bar.

Jack would not allow an apprentice to continue building the engine until he had inspected the main bearing stud split pin positions to ensure they were within one degree of each other, facing along the length of the engine. To add to the problem he would also insist on the split pins protruding beyond the castellated nut by exactly three-eighths of an inch, before being prised over to finally lock the nut. This meant cutting off small pieces from the standard length split pins and keeping the cut ends so that Jack could count them to ensure none had been inadvertently dropped into the crankcase, which could cause all sorts of problems. It goes without saying that all the split pins had to be inserted so that the 'legs' faced the back of the engine.

I suppose it instilled some discipline and taught apprentices how to make minor adjustment to threads, but on the whole it was a pretty meaningless exercise. However, since Jack was the master, we obeyed and just got on with it.

Moving on to my new master, a short, round little man named Harry, who lived on Richmond Road in Stechford, I realised how much rivalry there was between these engine fitters. Though Harry was in his 60s, he would always want to rebuild more engines during the week than his contemporaries. Consequently, he expected his apprentice to keep up with him. He never skimped on build quality, but his pace was relentless for a man of his age.

Harry had lost his wife a few years ago and was desperately lonely, so he took to writing letters to the 'Lonely Hearts' columns of the local newspaper in an attempt to meet someone new. He would often tell me that he was off that evening to meet someone who had made contact with him through the newspaper. Many of his dates never amounted to anything, except one.

I had moved on to another engine fitter, but I heard that Harry had taken a real shine to one of his correspondents, so much so that they had started going out with each other on a regular basis.

It seemed the friendship was developing well and Harry definitely had marriage in mind. However, when relating to us how much he enjoyed this woman's company, he also revealed how much money he was spending on her. One or two people commented, rather unkindly I thought, that Harry was probably being taken for a ride. Unfortunately their predictions were correct. After several months this woman apparently just disappeared and Harry, quite heartbroken, admitted that he had spent all his savings on her. Many of us felt sorry for him, but he was not put off. Within weeks, I heard that he had taken up with another of his correspondents from the newspaper.

I served three months with each of the four engine fitters and they all had some quirky way of working, which I accepted with alacrity. Notwithstanding Harry's love life and the pedantic ways of Jack and his fellow engine fitters. I gained a considerable amount of experience in overhauling a wide variety of engines, from single cylinder 100 cc two stroke petrol engines to huge six cylinder eight litre Gardner diesels.

Chapter 16
A DISTURBING INCIDENT

During my time in the overhaul shop an incident occurred which unnerved me for a time. I have already mentioned the five ton overhead crane that traversed the length and width of the overhaul workshop so that heavy loads could be lifted and deposited almost anywhere they were required. Well, the person who had to climb the steel ladder to gain access to the small driver's cab some 20 feet above our heads was a middle-aged Hungarian chap. He had escaped from Budapest when the Russians invaded Hungary on the 4th November 1956. The invasion produced something like 200,000 Hungarian refugees and some of them made their way to Britain. He had joined the staff of RMED as a labourer just a few months before me and had worked so well that the management added crane driving duties to his list of daily tasks. He was a really nice little bloke, always smiling and would talk to anyone at the drop of a hat. I suspect he wanted to improve his English, which on the whole was quite poor, but then my Hungarian wasn't too good either.

It was about ten past five on a Friday afternoon, I had been late cleaning the fitter's tools and putting them all away, so I was in a hurry to walk across the repair workshop to clock off and get home. As I dodged between all the parked vehicles, I heard a gurgling/coughing sound as if someone was choking. I stopped and listened again and sure enough, the sound was coming from behind one of the vehicles. I walked round the back of the truck and that's when I saw him. The little Hungarian was writhing and flailing about on the floor, hitting his hands and feet against the wheels of the trucks on either side of him. I wondered what on earth was going on and began to panic slightly. Moving towards him I called his name, but he made no response and it was then that I saw he was literally foaming at the mouth. Clearly he was having a fit of some sort. I tried to get him to lie on his side because I had read or heard that this was the thing to do if you came across a person having a fit. My effort was wasted because he just kept flailing around and it was impossible to keep him turned on his side. In something of a fluster, I moved to the front of the vehicle from where I could see Mr Goodman's office, hoping that he would still be sitting there. Luckily he was just putting his coat on to go home, so I ran closer to his office and shouted for him to come to where the Hungarian was lying.

The moment Mr Goodman saw the poor chap thrashing about on the floor he knew exactly what to do. He told me to go and get a piece of round wooden doweling from the chippie's shop so that he could put it in the man's mouth to stop him biting or swallowing his tongue. I rushed like a madman to the deserted carpenter's shop and after just a minute I was back showing Mr Goodman a piece of doweling about a foot long and half an inch in diameter. Mr Goodman forced the Hungarian's mouth open and told me to place the doweling between the man's teeth, but above his tongue. Having done that with some difficulty, Mr Goodman then restrained the Hungarian's flailing arms and asked me to grip his kicking feet. We held him there for several minutes before he calmed down. Once the Hungarian had come out of the fit, Mr Goodman told me to stay with him whilst he went to his office to phone for an ambulance. On his return, the foreman told me to go out of the main doors and wait in the yard for the ambulance to arrive. Twenty minutes later, the Hungarian was tucked up on a stretcher and being bundled into the back of the ambulance, which I had let into the workshop through the main doors. Mr Goodman gave the ambulance driver the Hungarian's personal details and, after seeing it off the premises, we both breathed a sigh of relief.

"Well done, Ken. He could have been in big trouble if you hadn't spotted him. Now go home and try to forget all about it," said the foreman with a smile.

The following Monday the little Hungarian reported for work and immediately came over to me in the overhaul shop to thank me. Somewhat embarrassed, I acknowledged his thanks and enquired what the problem had been. He thought for a moment and then said just one word somewhat hesitantly, "Epilepsy."

The hospital had prescribed some drugs to control the fits, so he was able to continue working and he was still there when I eventually left the employ of the railways, but his crane driving days were well and truly over.

Chapter 17
THE GEARBOX AND TRANSMISSION OVERHAUL WORKSHOP
January 1960 to July 1960

After finishing with the engine fitters, I moved across the workshop to the gearbox and transmission overhaul area, where every make and model of gearbox, rear axle and propeller shaft was repaired and refurbished. Many of the older heavy trucks utilised what were known as 'crash' gearboxes. These tended to be quite big, heavy units with large gearwheels that had to mesh with one another as the driver changed gear. To drive such a truck without the accompanying crashing sound from the gears required what was known as double-declutching to bring both gear wheels to the same peripheral speed so that they could engage silently.

Some drivers were not very skilled at this; consequently the damage to the gears inside the gearbox had to be seen to be believed. We also overhauled the latest synchromesh gearboxes that were fitted to the more modern trucks, small vans and the cars used by the senior RMED management. The van and car gearboxes were much smaller and compact and therefore didn't require so much manhandling during repair.

Many of the rear axles we dealt with were of the 'crown wheel and pinion' type and quite conventional, but some of the bus and heavy truck axles were of the 'worm and wheel' type. These required some real precision work to set the clearances correctly so that the bronze 'wheel' would not be ground away by the hardened steel 'worm'.

Some of the front axles we overhauled could be very difficult to handle, especially when trying to remove the swivel or king pins, around which the stub axle rotated to provide steering. The king pins were often seized solid into the axle beam and even after submersing the whole axle in the gunk tank for several days, it still required a sledgehammer, a steel punch and two people to force them out.

The front axle would be placed in a heavy-duty vice and the fitter, standing on the bench, would swing the sledgehammer whilst the apprentice (as ever was) gingerly held the steel punch over the head of the king pin with the longest pair of tongs he could find. After several heavy swipes with the sledge the pin might just ease out, if you were lucky. It was at times like this that some bright spark would walk by and comment on the 'precision engineering' going on in the axle department.

We overhauled prop-shaft yoke bearings like shelling peas and would often have a spurt for a couple of days to build up a stock, since prop-shafts used to 'sell' like hot cakes.

I really don't remember much more about my six months in this department or the two fitters who worked there and no further anecdotes spring to mind, so I must conclude that this part of my training went smoothly and without a hitch. Thank you anonymous fitters, everything you taught me must have stuck because I could still overhaul a gearbox and a rear axle, even today.

Chapter 18
A NOTE ABOUT NATIONAL SERVICE
(CONSCRIPTION)

There had been conscription to the armed forces on and off in the UK since 1916, largely to fulfil wartime requirements. However, due to the deterioration of relations between the Soviet bloc and the West after the Second World War and to enable peacetime conscription, the government formulated a new National Service Act (1948). It required all healthy young men between the ages of 18 and 21 to serve in one of the three branches of the armed forces for 18 months. The act became law on the 1st of January 1949.

In October 1950 the period of service was increased to two years because of the Korean War and Britain's involvement in it through the United Nations. There were exceptions and other conditions where cancellation or deferment of service could be applied. Apprentices serving a bona-fide indentured apprenticeship could (if they so wished) postpone their conscription to the armed forces until they had finished their time at the age of 21. This had to be formally applied for and proof that an apprenticeship was being served was required by the Ministry of Defence. By all the rules, I could have been called-up at any time after April 1960, unless granted deferment. Clearly I was deferred, but how this happened remains a mystery. To the best of my recollection I did not receive any government communications regarding national service or deferment; neither did my parents on my behalf. I must assume, therefore, that unless I did actually make an application and have forgotten all about it, the deferment was requested by The British Transport Commission (British

Railways) on behalf of all their apprentices. Though, here again, to the best of my knowledge there was never any discussion between me and my employer on this topic. As it turned out none of my generation of apprentices had to be conscripted since the government brought national service to a close on 31st December 1960, and the last British national serviceman was actually demobbed in May 1963 (the result of a deferment, no doubt).

Chapter 19
THE COMPLETE VEHICLE OVERHAUL WORKSHOP
July 1960 to April 1961

I was destined to spend nine months in the vehicle overhaul department before moving on to the vehicle servicing and repair side of the workshop. My master was a little Irishman (from the Republic) named Willy (William). He was about 30 years old and no taller than five feet, but he had the strength of a grizzly bear and a temper to match. He was an ardent gambler and would place bets on the horses every single day in the hope of hitting the jackpot. He employed mysterious (to me at least) formulae known as doubles and trebles and all sorts of wonderful computations and combinations to achieve his visionary jackpot, but I think at the end of the day the bookie was the only winner.

When we were at the workshop, Willy would wander over to the loco shed to place his bet with a chap there. However, if we were out and about road testing, for example, Willy would go to the bookmakers in whatever district of the city we happened to find ourselves. How he knew where all the bookies were was a complete mystery because in those days there were no well signed, brightly lit betting shops. Off-racecourse betting was illegal, so all these bookmakers that Willy used were operating beyond the law. I used to sit in the vehicle smiling as I watched Willy nod discreetly as he walked past the 'bookies runner' (who was there to warn of any patrolling policemen) and dodge quickly down the entry of an ordinary looking terraced house to reach the bookie's inner sanctum at the back.

Willy lived in a railway house next to the station in Coleshill, with his wife and children. I met his family on several occasions and his kids were great, very well behaved and well mannered. His wife was a really pleasant lady and a superb cook who could rustle up an excellent meal in no time at all.

One of Willy's favourite sayings, that he often used when we apprentices said rude things about his work or called him 'Paddy' simply to annoy him, was, "You English are not as sophisticated as I was initially informed back home. In fact I've discovered that you're just an ignorant load of useless bastards."

Notwithstanding the mickey-taking and the banter, we apprentices all got on well with Willy. I think it was because he was younger than all the other fitters and had a bit of the devil in him too.

One of the most challenging jobs we undertook was the complete overhaul of a road sweeper truck. I seem to remember that it was manufactured by Dennis and must have been one of the first they had ever made, it was so old. Some bright spark in the chief road motor engineer's office had decided that this road sweeper should be refurbished and used around the huge Lawley Street goods yard.

Willy and I nearly had fits when we saw this thing being towed into the workshop, because it had obviously been parked in some goods shed for about ten years, it was so dilapidated. We cleared the decks and set to dismantling it and sending the engine and transmission units for overhaul at the other part of the workshop. This left us with the cab and the bodywork containing all the rotating brushes, water jets and suction pipes for removing dirt and rubbish from the streets. To the rear of the chassis there was a water tank, a conveyor system and a container for all the sweepings. The cab was rusty, the chassis was rusty and all the sweeping mechanism was rusty too. The whole thing was only fit for the scrap heap.

"Go and get Mr Goodman to come and look at this heap of scrap," said Willy as he scratched his head.

I rushed off to Mr Goodman's office and asked him to come and see what we were expected to overhaul.

"Oh, my God, they must have gone mad in the office," was all he could say when Willy showed the foreman around the pile of junk that was our sweeper.

Mr Goodman told us to stop work on it until he had clarified things with the office. We busied ourselves with other work for a couple of days before the foreman came back to us.

"Yes, well, you just have to do the best you can," said Mr Goodman before disappearing back to his office.

Willy looked at me and said, "Well, what the hell are you waiting for? Get on with it," before bursting out laughing.

I won't bore the reader with the details of overhauling this monstrosity, but suffice it to say that it took us the whole nine months I was with Willy to obtain parts, manufacture parts and adapt parts from other more modern road sweepers to fit.

On the other hand, the engine and transmission units were overhauled quite quickly and they even found that many of the parts they required were actually in stock.

The major job entailed rebuilding the cab and bodywork from sheet steel and completely refurbishing the sweeping mechanism. What a nightmare. Naturally, when we were unable to work on the road sweeper, we busied ourselves with the other vehicles that had come in for overhaul.

When the sweeper was finally finished, I was almost ready to move on to the repair shop, so Willy allowed me the honour of starting the engine and driving the machine into the yard to test its ability to sweep. After some confusion, I got it sweeping reasonably well. With some further minor adjustments, Willy and I were driving around the yard next to the loco sheds leaving a cleanly swept area behind us and laughing our heads off. After several laps of honour and having the rubbish compartment cleared of the sweepings, we delivered the nightmare we had endured for nine months to the paint shop to be refinished in the carmine-and-cream British Railways' livery.

Despite the road sweeper job and others like it, I enjoyed every minute of my time with Willy. He taught me a lot and I had fun learning from him. There was never a dull moment in Willy's department, be it bouts of mickey-taking, serious political discussion (he tended to have socialist leanings, but he enjoyed capitalism to the full) or just larking about, he made coming to work a pleasure for all his apprentices. Thanks Willy, you were always the master, but also a good friend to me and many others too.

Chapter 20
TRAGEDY STRIKES

One of our apprentices was an older boy named Frank Riley, who lived in Smethwick. I had become friendly with him over the years and when he acquired an old MG Midget (M type); he asked me and one of my other friends, Frank Moore (referred to as Frank-M here to avoid confusion), if we would like to help him refurbish it at weekends. He told us that whilst he couldn't pay us for our labour, he would willingly supply all the food and drink for the day. Frank-M and I were delighted with the prospect of stripping such an iconic car and rebuilding it from scratch, so we agreed immediately.

Frank Riley was a tall young man of about 19, so he was a year ahead of Frank-M and me. He wore his hair in the style of Elvis Presley and loved the music that Elvis created. In fact, when Frank mimicked Elvis in voice and movement, as he often did, he actually began to look like him, such was the uncanny resemblance. Whilst Frank liked to joke around a lot, he was doing well in his studies and no one at the workshop doubted that he would make a good fitter when he finished his time.

Providing the weather was good on a Saturday morning, Frank-M, occupying the pillion seat, and I would motorcycle over to Smethwick where Frank lived with his widower father. Arriving very early, we would work all day on the MG in the little garage at the back of the house. Good to his word, Frank supplied us with a wonderful fry-up on our arrival in the morning, a lunch of doorstep sized sandwiches and all the mugs of tea we could handle. This went on for about three Saturdays and we made great progress in stripping, cleaning and reassembling the vehicle. None of us had any doubts that when it was finished, this old MG would look an absolute picture and perform like the sports car it was.

It must have been after the fourth Saturday at Frank's place working on the car that Frank-M and I returned to work on the following Monday to some absolutely devastating news.

It was mid-morning and Mr Goodman came over to where I was working and said, "Ken, listen, I have some bad news. Your friend, Frank, from Smethwick, his father found him dead in his bed this morning."

I heard the words all right, but I still blurted out, "What?"

Then the usual questions raced out of my mouth, but Mr Goodman could answer none of them except to say that according to his father, Frank had been accidentally gassed.

Naturally there was an inquest into Frank's death and we heard later that the coroner had determined that he had somehow accidentally turned on the gas tap to the gas fire in his bedroom before falling asleep. There was no suggestion of suicide, but if there had been I would not have believed such a thing in Frank's case. He was not the sort of person to even contemplate suicide.

Many older houses, my parents' house included, had gas fires in the bedrooms. Dad had taken these out of our house when I was born and had capped the gas pipes, which usually stuck out of the floor near the fireplace, to prevent such accidents. There was no North Sea Gas in those days, 'town gas' was produced at the local gasworks by 'cooking' coal and it was lethal if breathed in for any length of time. Furthermore, the gas fires then had no automatic safety device that cut off the gas in the event no ignition took place within a given time. If the gas tap was accidentally turned on and the fire was not ignited with a match, the gas would flow quite uninterrupted until the tap was turned off, with fatal consequences for anyone in the vicinity. There was also the danger of an explosion too.

Four of us apprentices, who had been close to Frank, along with a few of the fitters from the workshop, attended his funeral at a church in Smethwick, which I found very depressing. It was the first funeral I had ever been to and it felt unnatural to me that we should be witnessing the body of such a young man being placed into a hole in the ground. In my naive view, funerals were for really old people who had led full lives, not youngsters like Frank who had barely started to live.

Chapter 21
THE SERVICE AND REPAIR WORKSHOP
April 1961 to January 1962

After the trauma of Frank Riley's premature death and an exciting nine months working for Willy, my life returned to normal. A lot of the fitters in the service and repair shop were older men and quite set in their ways, so excitement was not on the agenda. There were exceptions, however.

My first master was a very tall, sophisticated chap of about 35; whose name, if I remember correctly, was Ronny. He was in charge of the private car repair and servicing, so it was considered quite an honour to work with him. He drove a superbly maintained, black 1939 SS Jaguar 100. In the summer months he would arrive at work with the top down, wearing a flat cap, white silk scarf, driving gloves, a sports jacket and a pair of grey flannel trousers. He really was quite the rake. It was rumoured that he had once been very rich, but had fallen on hard times. I didn't believe that story. I think he was simply a well spoken, well mannered and well educated man who had chosen his vocation freely and enjoyed it.

In all the years I knew him I had never seen him with dirty overalls. In contrast, by the time I had finished a week's work, my overalls could just about stand up on their own such was the quantity of grease and muck ingrained into them.

Ronny always dressed very smartly and wore a white shirt and dark tie under his overalls, which magically never ever became soiled. His shoes (no, he didn't wear toe protector boots like me and almost everyone else) were always clean and shiny too. How he managed it was nothing short of black magic because he wasn't a slacker, he worked just as hard as anyone else at the workshops.

The cars he serviced and repaired were those allocated to the management and were generally quite clean and tidy, as opposed to the commercial vehicles I had been used to overhauling. Despite a thorough steam cleaning before they came into the workshop, the commercial vehicles were still pretty grubby and the cabs could resemble the inside of a dustbin, such was the filth and detritus left there by some of the less fussy drivers.

During my time with the private car section, Ronny and I were required to service and repair about eight or ten cars, consisting of Humber Hawks Mark IV, at least one Humber Super Snipe Mark IV, a couple of Austin Cambridge A110 models and some Morris Oxfords Series VI.

Because they were manager's cars they had to be treated with care and attention, so we were required to use seat protectors and wing protectors when working on them. Furthermore, every single one of the cars was black in colour, which tended to show every tiny mark and blemish, so special care was always required.

It was interesting to work on cars after so many heavy commercial vehicles and the road test afterwards to ensure that everything was working properly, was a real treat. After removing our overalls, Ronny would drive with me sitting next to him imagining I was the chief road motor engineer as we drove out of the yard and on to the streets of Birmingham. If the weather was fine, we often took to the Coventry Road as far as the airport and then gave the cars a good blast along the A45 all the way to Coventry to blow the cobwebs away.

It was interesting to compare the engineering on these cars, which to me looked very flimsy and delicate, after the commercial vehicles I was used to. I enjoyed my time in the private car section and learned something about the sophisticated engineering and designs that modern cars were beginning to adopt.

After being spoilt for three months by what I called the 'miniature engineering' and the cleanliness of private cars, I was sent back to the more familiar, dirty old commercial vehicle service and repair section, 'real engineering' as I called it.

The RMED worked on the principle that there were just three types of commercial vehicle inspections.

'A Inspection'. This was a straight forward routine service of the vehicle after a certain mileage had elapsed.

'B Inspection'. This included an A Inspection, plus checking of all fluid levels and braking systems, again after a specified elapsed mileage.

Finally there was the 'C Inspection', which entailed the total overhaul of the vehicle chassis, engine, transmission and braking systems after an extended mileage.

Depending on how hard a vehicle was worked and what mileage it covered, the average goods yard Scarab could have up to four A Inspections and two B Inspections in a year, with a C Inspection every four or five years. However, we had one Scarab (I can still remember its stock number, 1066), which operated 24 hours per day at Lawley Street goods yard and received an A Inspection every week, a B Inspection every four weeks and a C Inspection every single year.

Our work in the service and repair shop entailed carrying out mainly A and B Inspections and running repairs. This included the renewing of brake shoes and drums. The brakes always needed frequent attention, especially on those vehicles that undertook local deliveries in the city. The stop-start pattern of city traffic played havoc with brake linings.

To ensure that all the brake drums were absolutely free of grease and oil before replacing them over newly fitted brake shoes, we often utilised the contents of the vehicle's fire extinguisher to clean them out. We called it Pyrene, after the company that made the small, hand-pumped, brass-bodied fire extinguishers fitted to all railway vehicles. However, the substance inside the extinguisher, which removed grease exceptionally well and evaporated quickly, was in fact Carbon Tetrachloride. This chemical is now known to cause liver failure and is therefore no longer used in fire extinguishers. Obviously, it was essential that the Pyrene extinguisher be topped up after its unorthodox use, and that was always the apprentice's job. Though I do wonder how many of those extinguishers were actually full when the vehicle left the workshop. Thankfully, we never experienced any vehicle fires in all the time I worked for the railways, so whether the extinguishers were full or not was never put to the test.

After carrying out the required repairs we would take the vehicle out for road test to bed-in and balance the brakes. We always ended up in either Landor Street or Garrison Street because both streets were long and straight, therefore ideal for brake testing.

New brake shoes need bedding-in before they work to their full efficiency, which entailed driving along the street and applying the brakes, gently at first, every 30 seconds or so. After 30 minutes the brakes would be noticeably more effective. At this point it was time to see that they were properly balanced by driving up to the legal limit (or perhaps just a bit faster) and slapping the brakes on hard and fast. Sometimes the brakes would be perfectly balanced and the vehicle would stop in a straight line. On other occasions the brakes would not be so well balanced and the vehicle would slew all over the road with one or two wheels locking up amid a plume of rubber smoke from the tyres. This latter occurrence frightened the life out of the motorists behind and those coming the other way and would often result in us being called all sorts of names by these startled drivers. Naturally we tried to carry out the tests when the road was free of traffic, but that was not always possible in a big city like Birmingham. Over the years, however, the local traffic came to avoid both Garrison Street and Landor Street during the daytime because they knew there would be railway vehicles driving up and down doing crazy things.

The winter of 1962-63 was one of the worst on record in the UK. Snow lay in the city for weeks and the temperatures were so low that the diesel-powered municipal buses stopped working as the freezing weather turned the fuel waxy, which tended to block the feed pipes. It caused us some real problems with our diesel trucks too.

Batteries don't operate well in low temperatures, so we often had to go along to the Lawley Street goods yard (the biggest in the city) plus other yards in the district to start dozens of stricken vehicles. The constant trekking back and forth during those six weeks of bad weather was really exhausting.

We would collect some slave batteries from the battery cage and put them in a little Ford van and do the tour of all the goods yards in the vicinity of Saltley. It would often take us most of the day to get everything moving; only having to repeat the whole operation again the following day because many of the goods yards did not have sufficient cover to protect the vehicles from the cold and frost.

The diesel vehicles would often suffer from fuel waxing (today, diesel fuel has anti-waxing additives to prevent this problem), so we would try to warm the fuel pipes and tanks by placing small kerosene-burning heaters underneath the fuel tank and in the engine compartment. After a couple of days of getting vehicles started, we managed to persuade the drivers to help themselves by wrapping old horse blankets (of which there were many in storage at Lawley Street, since they had only disposed of their last few hundred horses a short while ago) around the fuel tanks and the bonnets of their vehicles to keep out the cold.

One or two of the very old vehicles did not have electric starters, relying instead on pure muscle and a cranking/starting handle. If these were diesel-powered, and one or two were, then the starting problem became very acute and it would take the effort of two of us to get the engine going.

First we would place a kerosene burner under the fuel tank to dissolve the wax in the fuel and then we would place a similar burner, with the flame trap removed, under the sump of the engine to thin the engine oil a little. The railways used single grade, reclaimed engine oil in the SAE 30 and 40 ranges (called Silkolene), which could thicken-up like treacle in really cold weather. Thank goodness we have multi-grade oils these days.

After seeing to other, easier to start, vehicles we would return to the vehicle being 'warmed up' and one of us would be encouraged to 'volunteer' to turn the starting handle while the other operated the decompression valves with which all these hand-cranked diesels were fitted. Obviously it was always the apprentice who had to 'wind the handle'.

At a given signal I would start cranking the engine as fast as I could while my master placed the decompression valves on the engine to the full decompression position. Once I had the engine turning over at a reasonably steady speed, my fitter would drop the decompression valves to half decompression. When light coloured smoke started to appear at the exhaust, he would warn me, drop the valves to full compression and squirt a small amount of Ki-Gass (a mixture of diesel fuel and kerosene) into the air intake to assist combustion. If we were lucky, the engine would fire correctly and start. Sometimes, however, the engine simply kicked back and it would be necessary to let go of the cranking handle very smartly to avoid injury. One thing I learnt very quickly was to keep my thumb on the same side of the cranking handle as the rest of my fingers to prevent it being broken in the event of a kick-back.

On one particularly cold day there were so many diesels that required warming up, we ran out of kerosene burners and had to resort to lighting small wood fires under the engine sump to warm up the lubricating oil. On these occasions we would insist that the driver stood by with his fire extinguisher (wistfully hoping it had been topped up), just in case the flames got out of hand.

All this messing about could take quite a time and we often had the yard foreman breathing down our necks because he needed to have the truck loaded as soon as possible.

Yard foremen were the lords and masters of everything they surveyed; having total control over anyone and anything that had the temerity to enter their domains. That included railway shunting engines and their drivers, railway road vehicles and their drivers and most certainly any fitter and his snotty little apprentice from the road motor workshop.

"Can't you blokes work any faster? I've got thousands of parcels to get out today," was the usual cry.

If the man was reasonable, we would try to reassure him and he would usually go away, letting us get on with the business of keeping his yard moving. However, if he hung around making a nuisance of himself or became obstreperous and abusive (and they often did because they were under extreme pressure from their bosses to keep the parcels flowing), my master would sometimes instruct me to start packing the tools away, tell the foreman his fortune and begin walking towards our little van saying, "If you can do what we're doing any bloody faster, be my guest, mate."

That usually shut them up and made them go away.

We worked extremely hard that winter and kept things running as best we could, but it was a hard slog, despite there being three or four pairs of 'cold starters' from the other district workshops helping us. I can remember getting home in the evenings during that period feeling cold, miserable and absolutely exhausted.

Chapter 22
I GET MARRIED

In September 1961, I married Judith, my fiancée of almost two years, at All Saints' Church in Albert Road, Stechford. One of my fellow apprentices, Malcolm, acted as my best man. My own sister, Christine, and my wife's sister, Lynne, acted as bridesmaids. At this time I was earning about six pounds per week and my wife was earning about ten, so I was a 'kept' man for a few years before I finished my apprenticeship and began to earn the full rate.

We lived in a really nice flat in Victoria Road, just opposite my parents' house. Much later on we moved out to the pleasant greenery of Marston Green, close to the railway station. We had three children, Stephen in 1966, Stuart in 1969 and Abigail in 1980.

Over the years, largely as a result of me securing better jobs, we moved several times, residing in West Africa for a number of years before moving back to the UK and living in Bedfordshire, Lancashire and Berkshire. Sadly my wife died in 2003 and though I miss her and think about her every single day, I am pleased to see that she lives on through our children.

THE FINAL FIFTEEN MONTHS
(January 1962 to April 1963)

Again I record some of the headlines that appeared in the newspapers during this period of my apprenticeship.

April 1962
Stirling Moss injured in crash at Goodwood.

May 1962
Coventry's new Cathedral opens.

January 1963
Hugh Gaitskell, Labour leader, dies aged 56.

March 1963
Dr Beeching publishes his report on the future of the Railways.

So that we gained experience of working in the 'sticks' our apprenticeship schedule demanded that we spend at least fifteen months at the district workshops, which weren't so well equipped, catering only for day-to-day running repairs and minor servicing (A Inspections).

Chapter 23
THE DISTRICT WORKSHOPS
January 1962 to April 1963

My first district workshop was just around the corner from Saltley, in Curzon Street. I remember being quite impressed as I motorcycled past what remained of Philip Hardwick's (1792-1870. Architect to the London and Birmingham Railway Company) magnificent Roman inspired entrance to the passenger station, which was opened in 1838. Turning my motorcycle to the left, I passed through one of the ornate arches in the Romanesque style wall, which ran for two hundred yards along the street from the station entrance. Behind this wall was the Curzon Street road motor workshop. The foreman was expecting me and, after telling me where to park my bike, he invited me in.

The workshop was very small and because of the constant stream of traffic in and out, the doors were open for most of the day. Fine in summer, but it was January and the place was freezing.

The foreman was a youngish chap about 35 years old with ginger hair. He told me I would be working with a much older man named, Fred. After introducing me to Fred, the foreman went back into his office at the top of a set of steps and settled down to his paperwork. I learned later that he had an electric fire under his desk and was very comfortable, despite the freezing weather.

Fred was from Northumberland and had moved to Birmingham 20 odd years ago to find work. He lived in a nice semi-detached house on Stechford Lane near the Beaufort Cinema and The Fox & Goose pub. He was a nice old chap and I got on with him very well because he trusted me to do whatever he had asked me to do with little or no interference.

Most of the work consisted of running repairs and small servicing jobs, such as oil changes, tune ups and brake adjustment. Since Curzon Street was primarily a goods yard, there were dozens of Scarabs to be looked after with the occasional Karrier Bantam tractor unit or Commer and Austin van thrown in for good measure.

Amazingly we had a chippie at Curzon Street, but his main occupation, apart from the usual renewal of floorboards in the Mechanical Horses and Scarabs, was renewing the domed fibreglass fronts fitted to the Scarabs. These were very vulnerable and he would often be engaged in fitting at least one or two every day.

His name was Frank Smith and he lived in Selly Oak near the Ariel motorcycle factory. He was about 60 years old, quite plump and had snow-white hair. He owned a magnificent BSA 350cc (B31) motorcycle, which shone like a new pin. This was no surprise since he spent most of his lunch times cleaning it. If it had rained on his way to work, he would wipe the machine down as soon as he arrived, then at lunch time polish it up to a high sheen. Naturally we talked about motorcycles because I parked my rather scruffy-looking Tiger Cub in the same small storage area that he used.

It didn't take him long to persuade me to undertake some repairs to his BSA in my lunch breaks. He would buy the parts and I would fit them. He was very generous and always insisted on paying me at a decent rate, so the arrangement was mutually beneficial.

One day I had to call upon him to do me a big favour. I had just finished servicing and adjusting the brakes on a Scarab and had decided to take it for a road test, but only around the yard. The cobbled yard was quite small and always crowded with vehicles awaiting our attention, so the available 'test track' was very narrow and circular in shape. I drove the Scarab around a couple of times to be satisfied that everything was all right and then headed back to the workshop.

As I have mentioned, the Scarab was a three-wheeled vehicle, so the mechanically operated brakes were fitted to the rear wheels only. When the vehicle was being driven solo (without a trailer) there was virtually no weight on the rear axle at all, consequently the rear brakes would lock up at the drop of a hat. Putting it bluntly, the Scarab, driven solo, couldn't really stop in an emergency and behaved quite erratically when braking on wet cobbles. However, since the vehicle had a top speed of only 30 mph and was almost exclusively driven with a trailer attached that also had mechanically operated brakes (there was a special mechanism on the trailer coupling that operated via the footbrake in the cab), the ministry of transport must have thought it was OK.

On rounding the last bend, I saw something directly in front of me and slammed the brakes on. The vehicle, being solo, locked up and skidded slap-bang into the back of the trailer of a tractor unit whose driver had suddenly decided to stop to light his cigarette. The fibreglass front of the Scarab shattered into pieces and looked a real mess. There was no other damage to my vehicle and virtually no damage to the trailer I had hit. In fact, the driver didn't even bother to get out; he simply drove on once his Woodbine was alight.

My difficulty was that the goods foreman wanted the Scarab back that afternoon and now it was only fit for the workshop again. I parked the Scarab in the far corner of the yard out of sight and called Frank over to ask him if he would change the front cowl quickly and not tell our foreman. He looked at me and smiled before telling me gleefully that I was now in his debt.

Changing the fibreglass front on a Scarab was really quite easy since the new part was supplied already painted in railway carmine colour and all Frank had to do was drill holes where it bolted on to the metal cab. However, it required a knack to get it to fit correctly and our chippie had mastered that many years ago.

Frank completed the work in time for the goods foreman to have his Scarab back in good order. However, as soon as the vehicle had been handed over, Frank demanded (in a non-threatening manner, of course) that I tune his motorcycle at the first opportunity, completely free of charge. Knowing I had been well and truly 'blackmailed', I set about re-tuning the carburettor on his bike the following lunch time. It wasn't much of a price to pay, there was very little adjusting to do, the bike was running perfectly and had been for a long time. We laughed about it afterwards and our foreman never did find out that I had crashed the Scarab.

As time moved on, I discovered that the foreman was very religious, nothing wrong with that if you like that sort of thing, but he did tend to try and lecture young men like me. I would always find an excuse to cut the conversation short once he started on the religious stuff and I think he got the message because after a few weeks he stopped raising the subject.

Towards the end of my six months at Curzon Street, I did an increasing amount of my work unsupervised and soon became very comfortable in taking responsibility for everything I did. When my time came to leave, I was toasted in tea by all the men in our small mess room in the goods yard and wished good luck for the future.

My next posting was to the workshop in the goods yard at Lawley Street. I really don't remember too much about it except that we had plenty to do, so the days just seemed to run into one another. As I have already pointed out, Lawley Street was the biggest goods yards in the city and it operated 24 hours per day, seven days per week, moving parcels and freight all over the Midlands and beyond. To call it busy would be an understatement. We worked from morning till night servicing and repairing vehicles a fast as we could. No matter how quickly we worked, the goods foreman was never satisfied. I finally reached the conclusion that he really thought we were more of a hindrance to his operation than an asset and would have happily banned us from his goods yard if he could. He simply didn't seem to understand the importance of servicing and repairs to his vehicles at all.

It was during my Lawley Street posting that I was directed to attend British Railways' driving school at Sutton Coldfield, which was situated in the large station yard quite close to Sutton Park. I already had a full car driving licence which entitled me to drive vehicles up to 7.5tons (the rules have changed several times since the 1960s), but the railways liked their drivers to go through their own driving test, which was designed to take into account the operations that railway drivers were expected to undertake.

The school was run by a man who had been a fitter at the Saltley workshops until he was involved in an accident there which damaged his right hand so badly it had to be amputated. Thereafter, he wore a prosthetic hand that he covered with a black leather glove. The story goes that the RMED management, being well aware that he was not entirely to blame for the accident, moved him to Sutton when he had recovered so that he could take over the driving school and maintain his rate of pay.

Everyone who drove railway vehicles, permanently or casually, was required to attend for two weeks, as I recall. Most of the tuition involved the handling of the ubiquitous Scarab. Therefore, a majority of the time was spent reversing this three-wheeled workhorse, plus other four-wheeled articulated vehicles, whilst trying to control the direction of the attached trailer with pin-point accuracy.

I can remember the instructor shouting at me, "Bloody hopeless, do it again. Do it again," each time I failed to reverse the trailer to exactly where he wanted it.

I must have completed the course with good marks because I was awarded my railway licence immediately, which not only entitled me to drive railway vehicles on the public roads, but also on railway property, a very important distinction. The fact that I had been driving railway vehicles ever since I obtained my regular ministry of transport licence was neither here nor there.

I moved on to Aston workshops after six months at Lawley Street, but my memories of that place are now somewhat vague, but I do remember how small and pokey the workshop was and freezing cold too, even in the summer. I know I didn't stay there more than a couple of weeks.

After Aston, I was ordered to work at a new workshop that had only just been opened in Garrison Street. It was a really modern building with proper heating and fine workshop facilities too. The mess room, locker rooms and toilets were sparkling with cleanliness and the water in the taps actually came out hot every time they were turned on. I absolutely loved the place.

Chapter 24
I FINISH MY TIME

I completed my remaining three months or so at Garrison Street and eleven days after officially finishing my time, the foreman, Mr Bathurst, casually delivered (to be fair, unknowingly) my apprenticeship certificate to me in a scruffy old internal envelope. I opened it and looked at the certificate thinking, *so is this all I get after six long years of service and low wages?*

It was a single sheet of white paper about eight inches by ten inches with 'Certificate of Apprenticeship' printed across the top and my details typed into the blank spaces. It was signed by the chief road motor engineer, a chap called Brown, whom I had never met.

Mr Bathurst had no idea what was in the envelope and when I showed him what it was he said, "The miserable buggers, they should have made a show of this. Never mind Ken, I'll get some cakes and we'll have a bit of a celebration in the mess room at lunch time."

True to his word, the foreman came into the mess room at lunch time, handed cakes to everyone and told them that I had completed my apprenticeship. After a lot of cheering and mickey-taking, they all toasted me in tea and then dragged me to The Railway, a pub just across the road in Lawley Street, near the railway bridge. They bought me a pint of M&B (Mitchell's and Butler's) mild (I think it cost about tenpence (4p) in those days) and toasted me properly.

Naturally my wife and I, plus my parents, brothers and sister had celebrated my 21st birthday at home some days before and so the spontaneous gesture by the men at Garrison Street was the icing on the cake. It was really nice of them and I appreciated their kindness.

As I mentioned, the facilities at Garrison Street were far superior to those at Saltley, so when asked what I wanted to do, I elected to stay at the Garrison Street workshop. There was good reason for me to make that decision, other than the modernity of the facilities. The management had recently introduced a time and motion pilot scheme which enabled a fitter working constantly at a steady pace to earn up to 30% on top of his weekly rate. Basically, all routine jobs (such as removing an engine, overhauling a gearbox or carrying out a specific service) were timed and if the fitter completed all these tasks in the time allotted he would earn his weekly rate. However, if the work was carried out more quickly, then a bonus was earned. This could be quite a boost to a fitter's weekly wages and, not unnaturally, it attracted a lot of attention.

Talking of weekly wages, I naturally expected to be paid the full fitter's rate of £10-4s (£10.20) per week (£195 at 2016 values), immediately following the completion of my apprenticeship.

"Not so," said the accountant when I queried the first wage packet received after finishing my time, which was two shillings (10p) short.

"You were told when you signed your apprenticeship papers that you would have to serve as a journeyman for 12 months after finishing your time," he added rather superciliously.

I'm sure they did tell me, but I must have forgotten, so I had to soldier on for a year, two shillings per week below the full rate.

Fortuitously, the bonus scheme operating at Garrison Street more than made up for the shortfall in my wages. I was regularly earning 30% more, so I was least concerned.

My year as a journeyman passed very quickly and as the time study team progressed with the pilot scheme, I was timed on many occasions doing certain jobs on the wide variety of the vehicles we serviced and repaired. Finally, they released the bonus scheme to all the workshops in the region and the change was almost tangible. Work was finished more quickly and efficiently, and the men earned more than they had ever done so in the past. It was a great success and benefited both management and labour for a change.

The only negative comment from almost everyone was, "Why didn't they introduce it sooner?"

After my year as a journeyman was over, I was allocated my own apprentice. His name was Martin. He was a very polite and likeable young man and had just finished his time in the stores and the cages at the Saltley workshops, so this was his first time dealing with actual vehicles. He made mistakes of course, as we all did, but I managed to point out his errors and get him to set them straight without quite so much of the swearing and blustering that my previous masters had used on me.

He once filled a Fordson diesel engine with lubricating oil right to the top; you could see it in the rocker cover if you took the oil filler cap off. After some reflection, I decided that I really couldn't say much to him because I had said, "Fill the engine with oil."

I should have realised that he had never filled an engine before and shown him how to use the dipstick to determine the correct level. We simply drained the excess oil out of the engine and no real harm was done. Lessons learnt on both sides, I think.

We didn't work together for very long because a couple of months later I was promoted to chargehand. Consequently, I never saw Martin again, but I hope he was able to finish his apprenticeship and make good progress in his chosen vocation.

Within days of my promotion (with a new wage rate of £12-4s per week [£12.20] plus average bonus), I was sent to the wilds of the Black Country (places such as Wednesbury, Walsall and Quarybank) to carry out relief duty for those chargehands and foremen sick or on leave. What an experience that was, but my training came to the fore and served me well, even though I found it difficult to understand some of the fitters due to their very heavy Black Country accents.

After about six months of relief work, which also included my old stomping grounds at Curzon Street and Lawley Street, I was found a permanent position at the Coventry workshop. Yes, I was literally, 'Sent to Coventry'. This was fine and I got along with all the men quite happily, but the railways were losing goods traffic to the private road hauliers at a phenomenal rate.

Consequently, the railway vehicle fleet was being scrapped faster than ever before and new vehicle acquisitions were drying up too.

Time for a move, I thought.

Chapter 25
I LEAVE THE RAILWAYS

In 1965 I managed to get a job with Girling Brakes (part of the mighty Lucas group) at their engineering development centre in King's Road, Tyseley; almost next door to the loco sheds I had first visited eight years previously with my father. I was employed as a technical assistant in the commercial vehicle brake development department for a year, earning £17-10s (£17.50) per week and later promoted to assistant development engineer, earning £19 per week (£329 at 2016 values). I really enjoyed my time at Girling and learnt an awful lot about commercial vehicle braking systems and their design. However, I missed the variation that a busy workshop provided and began looking for something in the supervisory side of that business.

In April 1967, I found myself boarding a plane at Heathrow destined for Nigeria, having secured the position of service manager with a Birmingham based company (their head office was in Hagley Road) called Bewac (British [Engineering] West Africa Corporation) on a salary of £36-15s (£36.75) per week (£612 at 2016 values). The company was the sales, service and parts agent in West Africa for Leyland, Albion, Scammell, Rover, Land-Rover, Triumph, Rolls-Royce and Massey Fergusson agricultural equipment. But that is an entirely different story, which you can read all about in my memoir entitled, *The Up-Country Man: A personal account of the first one hundred days inside secessionist Biafra.*

Chapter 26
WAS IT ALL WORTH IT?

The short answer is, "Yes." My six years as an apprentice and one year as a journeyman were well worth it. What I would call, *'Time Well Spent'*.

I learnt so much from those sometimes quirky, taciturn and awkward old men at the RMED workshops. They gave their knowledge freely, without reservation and it had boundless value. There were no computers or automated mechanisms to assist with the work for these men; a first class job all depended on their knowledge and personal skill, which they had in abundance. All I had to do as an apprentice was to soak it up and support it with the theory that was imparted by the technical college. A great opportunity was there and, thankfully, I had the good sense to recognise it and grab it with both hands.

The skills and knowledge I absorbed like a sponge from those men (which I then supplemented by further academic study after serving my time) stood me in good stead for the whole of my working life, which, I would modestly say, turned out just fine.

My job with Bewac saw me overseeing the service workshops in Nigeria for a year. After that I was promoted to branch manager, running the company's sales and service outposts in remote areas of that country, often with no other European working at the branch.

When I eventually returned to the UK, I secured employment as an overseas service engineer at Rover in Solihull for a year or two. Later, during the late 1970s and early 80s, I transferred to British Leyland International and then to Leyland Truck and Bus, working in Africa again, the Middle East and the Far East. During my last 20 years, before retiring in 2004, I was the director of research at 'Thatcham' (The Motor Insurance Repair Research Centre), researching advanced repair methods, improved safety levels and the electronic security of modern motor vehicles.

The extensive international travel associated with my work resulted in my meeting and working with so many interesting and impressive people who were similarly engaged in senior positions within the motor industry throughout the world. In fact, I am still in touch with some of those people today and I am very proud to call them my friends.

My working life has been so varied and such a privilege for me that as I sit typing this manuscript, here in 2016, I can hardly believe it all actually happened. It had started with my late father insisting that I become an apprentice, and for that I must express my heartfelt thanks for his fatherly wisdom and foresight. Furthermore, I shall forever be in debt to those skilled men, now long gone, at the RMED workshops, who taught me so much and set me firmly on the road to success.

The apprenticeship I undertook with British Railways from 1957 to 1963 was one of the best in the country for its depth and range of vehicles and plant that were encompassed by the scheme. I doubt we shall ever see the like again because the golden age of real apprenticeships has long gone, leaving the young men and women of today all the poorer for it, in my view.

The British Transport Commission has gone. British Railways, as an entity, has gone and so has the Road Motor Engineers Department. There is no trace of the workshops in Duddeston Mill Road, neither is there any trace of the Saltley loco sheds. Everything has gone, as have all the district workshops too. The only structure left to remind me of my past life as a proud railway apprentice is the driveway (where I learnt that there was more to chocking the wheels of a 10 ton mobile crane than meets the eye) leading up the slope from Duddeston Mill Road to where the RMED workshops were once situated. It can still be seen when entering Duddeston Mill Road from Adderley Road. It's on the left hand side just before the low railway bridge that carries the main Birmingham to Derby railway line.

Printed in Great Britain
by Amazon